ALL ABOUT THE BOY

BY STEPHANE RAYNOR

The information and personal images in this book are based on materials supplied to the publisher by the author. While every effort has been made to ensure its accuracy, Pro-actif Communications does not under any circumstances accept responsibility for any errors or omissions. The copyright with regards to all contributions remains with the originator.

© Words by Stephane Raynor.

A catalogue record for this book is available from the British Library.

First Edition 2018

First published in Great Britain in 2018 by Carpet Bombing Culture.

An imprint of Pro-actif Communications

www.carpetbombingculture.co.uk

Email: books@carpetbombingculture.co.uk

© Carpet Bombing Culture. Pro-actif Communications

ISBN: 978-1-908211-65-1

CARPET
BOMBING
CULTURE

"IT'S MY HEROIN... WE CREATED IT AND I LIVE IT EVERY FUCKING DAY OF MY LIFE."
STEPHANE RAYNOR

This is the true story behind the founder of the iconic London fashion label 'BOY' told by the man himself - Stephane Raynor. Packed with punk attitude and original photography, buy a ticket and take the ride. Join Raynor on a journey through a life less ordinary - lived in a tireless pursuit for THE NEW.

Artist, innovator, designer, anarchist, hedonist, maverick, Raynor lives like he means it. The guy behind the guy behind the guy - he was there man... fomenting and agitating in the background of punk, new romantic, acid house, you fucking name it.

Stephane Raynor is so far ahead of his time there are rumours he came here from the future of outer space to liberate us from bland culture. The spirit of world history chose him, like Napoleon, to destroy the old world. Either that, or he's the most EPIC BLAG ARTIST of all time. He's not sure.

BUT DON'T GO THINKING THIS IS A FUCKING HISTORY BOOK.
This is a future book. The only hope for a life worth living in the most boring millennium of human history so far. This is a blueprint. Pick through the entrails of Raynor's 'career' to read the portents of that which cometh next. Do it now. Before history spits you out like flavourless chewing gum.

BOY LONDON - the eagle came to him in a dream. It told him it would soon take over the world. IT DID.

A VISION OF A WORLD where ordinary people can live like pop stars.

Put his book on your coffee table. Wear his shit. You will definitely get laid. And you'll deserve it.

Patrick Potter

Introduction

I'm an addict, a maverick, a master of deception, a troublemaker, an upsetter, an agitator, an originator of style over substance. I break the rules, I create, I provoke confrontation, I have an explosive imagination. Some call me a genius, others say I have the air of assured command, some think I'm a chancer. My followers say I've stayed true to my beliefs and have never sold out. Those who know me say I'm quiet and unassuming, almost shy. Maybe I'm all of those things.

I am Stephane Raynor, and from my control pad somewhere in underground London, I became the boy behind BOY.

This is my book, about my life. A never-ending story of paranoia, Punks, pills and pop stars, fashion, fame, fans and fucking with the establishment.

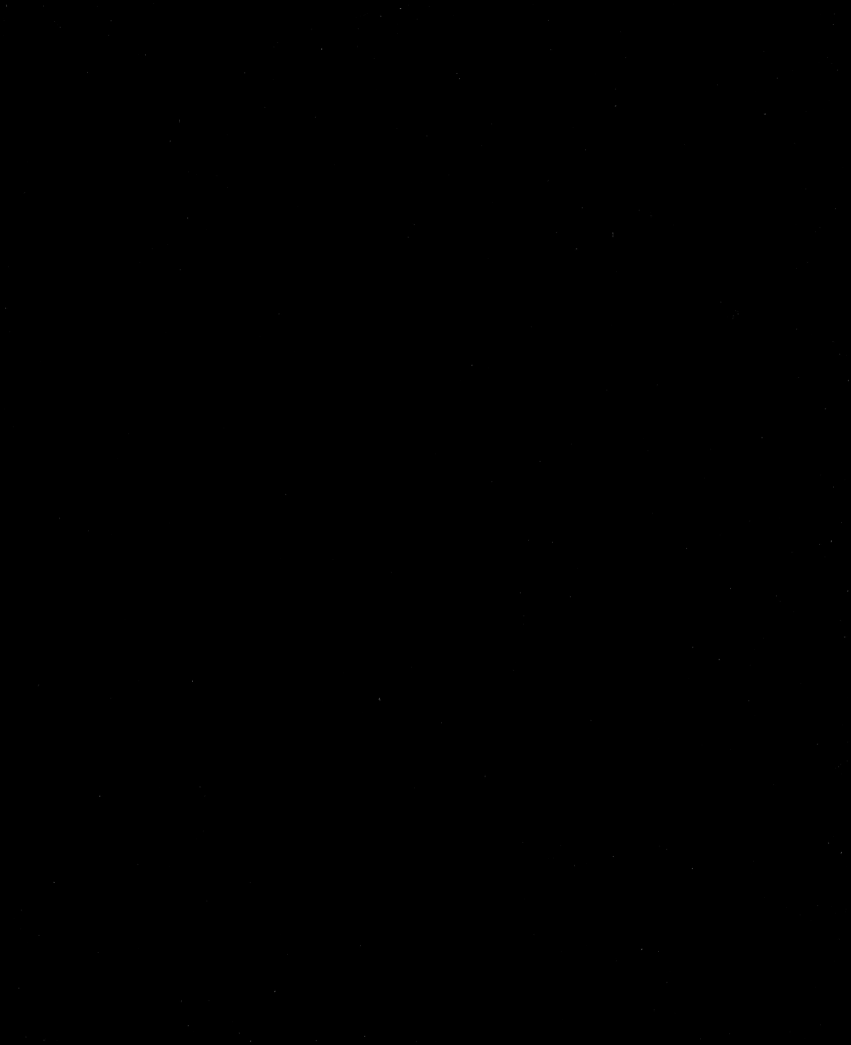

1960s

Origins

If someone said rewind your life and do it again I wouldn't change my start in Leicester. I wouldn't actually change a fucking thing about my life, I've loved every minute of it. I was the perfect age to see the Beatles explode on to the world stage, to be there when LSD and the Hippie movement happened, to find myself an instigator of Punk, then go on to create fashion chaos and be a part of every youth movement to come since. What a great fucking time to live.

I grew up on the bomb sites left over from The Second World War. Street after street of back-to-back houses with only an outside privy. The streets were dark and damp with no more than one rusty old black car or a motorcycle and sidecar parked up. Things only started to get more interesting for me when the local boozer began playing Blue Beat music for its new black immigrant patrons.

I never really fitted in though, and often felt as though I had been beamed down from another planet, I was on my own. When I was a young teenager there was an older girl I liked the look of who lived in one of the houses a few along from mine. She had a beehive hairstyle, you know the look, just like The Ronettes - only she was white and instead of being a muse of the great Phil Spector, she worked at the chippy on the corner a few streets away. I would queue up for chips on a Friday night and observe her, but she was never going to give a fuck about me, I was a nobody and as she was too busy eyeing up the Teddy Boys. I knew that for her to notice me I would have to become a Teddy Boy too. I went up the high street in Leicester one Saturday and bought myself a Gene Vincent style red and black striped cap and a snaffle tie. This was the moment I discovered the power of fashion, from that day on the girl in the chip shop smiled and started to say hello.

The power of pop music was transcending everything around me, I had the hair, I had girls, I had a guitar so I guess I had the look but I was shy. I learned to drive and bought a car, that was an important move and it shaped my life. I felt like I was part of those American movies where the kids would pull up in a cool American car at some hamburger joint or drive-in and they'd go drag racing and hang out with girls on roller skates. I'd go to the cinema to watch classic movies like The Girl Can't Help It and Rock Around the Clock and I'd watch as the Teddy Boys ripped up the seats and tore down the furnishings, rioting as Rock Around the Clock blasted out. I was desperate to be a part of it. I went to see Elvis in his first movie, Love Me Tender. I was sitting in the back row with the Teddy Boys. It wasn't quite the American dream but it was the start of the British sub-culture and not long after it became just as important if not more so with bands like The Beatles, The Kinks and The Stones.

Like the Beat Poets before me in 1950's America I had always felt drawn to the counter-culture and the abstract. I didn't even really know what it was or what it meant but I knew a few beatniks and I started hanging out in an arts café in Leicester where they played jazz and read poetry. I was part of the early teenage set and I could tell we were entering a powerful new world. I felt drawn to the Avant Garde but I wanted to think and create for myself, I needed to explore things that had never been done before so I packed away my Thelonious Monk and Miles Davis albums and concentrated instead on this new energy. I wanted to hang around with the misfits, the abstract personalities, kids from the streets like me who had fallen out with formal education, I was playing it by ear.

We are the Mods

My life really began to make sense though when I became a Mod. My mates and I were sharp and we ruled the streets. We took no prisoners and nobody could come between us. Once a Mod always a Mod. If we went to a club in my car the girls we hung around with at the time were made to travel in the boot because us guys were 'the faces' and therefore we were the ones that had to be seen.

I was surrounded by Mod girls in those days, loads of them, it was like being a rock star. They all knew the registration plate of my car and would look out for it on the streets. We didn't care about the music scene or the bands in Leicester, we were too cool for all that. We were all about the pubs and the dance floors but most of all we wanted to be the sharpest fucking dressers in town. Getting dressed and ready for the weekend was a really big event. It meant a trip to Burton's the Tailor or Austin Reed. Sometimes we'd head down the newly opened M1 to London's Petticoat Lane or Carnaby Street. Every so often I'd get a suit tailor made, then we'd wear our new gear out that evening strutting our stuff at The Scene or The Flamingo in Soho.

Leicester actually had a pretty decent scene for Mods, there were places to hang out where I could hook up with girls and take drugs. My car was really cool, it was an electric blue gull wing Ford Classic, so we had wheels and could venture further afield to towns like Derby, Nottingham and Sheffield. As it was my car I would select who came with me and I only chose the sharpest of the Leicester Mods. When we pulled up outside the clubs the car was star of the show, all the girls wanted to hang out in it and my old Ford Classic became an extension of the clubs. We took Purple Hearts, Double Dexedrine and anything else we could get hold of.

I'd been going to London to push drugs and go clubbing as any decent kingpin did back in those day. But my Mod hair had started to grow a bit wild and my mohair suit slightly tired looking. I was changing my look, morphing into something new. I was conscious that I had to kick down some new doors so I started to look rougher around the edges, more dishevelled, as a friend said, "you look like that cat Dylan". I had been turning into a Hippie without realising. There's always been some kind of shit going on in my head that made me want to delve into the next thing. For me, the Mod era was over, the edges were blurring. My music preference and my fashion style were changing, I started to drop soul music and Motown in favour of the new emerging bands like Cream, Blind Faith, Yes, Deep Purple, Jimi Hendrix, Traffic, Clapton and Rory Gallagher and I went to as many live gigs as possible. Every band that was worth seeing, I was there. My mind was expanding and Leicester had started to bite back, I knew that if I didn't split fast then I would be there forever.

This town ain't big enough

During my final days in Leicester me and my friend Will English were preoccupied with collecting stuff. We were stockpiling American tin cars, old juke boxes, robots, ray guns, ephemera objects and the like. Beatles shit, early pop annuals and anything to do with the 50's, Teddy Boy clothes, winkle pickers and painted ties. We stashed it all in a lock up that we rented for a few bob, I would circumnavigate towns and buy stuff for almost nothing, we were the salmon swimming against the current. We had no idea why we were doing it, it's just that we could and it was so cheap why wouldn't we! It was time to bust loose and get out though, I had a vision that there was a bigger life somewhere else and I didn't want to drown in my hometown. I left my dog, my girlfriend and my friends behind, got in my car and drove down to London.

I found myself the perfect flat on the famous Abbey Road, an entire floor of a building and it was dirt-cheap. Back then, like Earls Court, it was an area that the Hippies and the underground youth inhabited so it suited me just fine. I had three giant beasts of American cars, a Chevy, a Caddy and a Plymouth Satellite. They took up the whole fucking street! I brought down as much gear as I could and stored it in all corners of the flat. The stuff was everywhere.

During this time, I had an old Leicester mate now living in London. He was a photographer called David Parkinson known as Parko. We'd been in a band together in Leicester and he'd left for London some time earlier. He was a shacked up with a chick in Regents Park. I was hanging out with him much of the time and he was collecting the same kind of gear as me. He had to edit his collection though as his girlfriend didn't like the mess. He had bags of style and a great eye. We started going around London markets together.

Brick Lane was my entrée into this world. The 'Lane' was very reminiscent of the old days, with plenty of dodgy characters still hanging around. Gone were the monkeys and the organ grinders, but there were still pets for sale – birds, rabbits and other stuff, all illegal these days. When night time came around the underworld of the East End slid out from who knows where. There were men in their dirty old raincoats, streetwalkers, prostitutes old and young and working girls in thigh high boots and latex. Whether in Rome or Paris, like the Italian and French films, no night scene would be complete without "Les Girls" just like in the Fellini movie 'Roma'.

Parko and I would head to the Brick Lane Market every Sunday. We'd bump into Bikers with greased back hair, wearing leathers and the Teddy Boys digging through crates of 45's and 78's and buying Gene Vincent albums for a few pennies. There were only a few faces back then, they were wearing Edwardian drape jackets, bootlace ties and brothel creepers and they were buying all this stuff up. At the markets in Walworth Road and East India Docks we saw nobody, so we bought there like crazy.

I spent much of my time going back and forth from London to Leicester buying, going to gigs, living with various girlfriends, watching the world change. During this time there was still a cool scene back home so I would drive there by night, I've always loved night driving. I'd still hang out with my old Leicester mates who'd hit the Pink Floyd scene by then. We would sit around listening to music, doing LSD. There were always girls around; I guess it was our 'happening.'

When I was back in Leicester one particular weekend I decided to contact a friend of mine that had a shop near the university and student digs area. I thought I could use his set up as a way to sell some of my stuff and I ended up taking half the space from him. I had a girlfriend called Helen at the time and she ran the shop for me and I would be there from time to time to bring stock over and make plans. I guess those clothes would now be described as vintage, anyway the students were totally getting it. It was making me some decent dosh so I was able to spend most of my time on stock buying trips and living it up in London.

a while but it was
ew I needed to be
stock had happened
d wearing gold lame
k quiffs doing their
e Stones played Hyde

Park and I witnessed
marching through cr
crowd were glammir
Underground, Roxy
emerging, the Summ
was time to move or

s 'BOY' store provided the o
Westwood's Seditionaries in
inal bondage trousers and b
h slogans that challenged t
les of the status quo to go w
cked early Punk Rock group
ation X' groups so, not only
ed fuel the music revolution
nd and mentor... Rock on St

lest "club" in town, where
ent factions became more

1970s

Rock around the clock

So here I was with all this stock spread out between London and Leicester. I had managed to accumulate space helmet TV's, crates of vintage vinyl and books, jukeboxes and piles of Rock and Roll clothing. As always, I had no idea what do with it all plus I was mentally and emotionally moving away from the shop and my whole setup in Leicester. I was looking for a new door to open and a way to make some quick cash. I kicked things off by renting a stall on Portobello Road every Friday, which was market day. That kept me in readies but I knew it wasn't enough, I had to push things further. By this time Parko was freelancing for Club International magazine and one day he suggested we go and take a look at Tommy Roberts' boutique Mr Freedom on Church Street, Kensington. He'd been commissioned to do a photoshoot and needed to borrow some cool clothes. We hung around there for a bit, chose some great pieces then headed to another shop that Tommy owned on the King's Road and was renting out to the Paradise Garage people. We bagged up more cool stuff there, jumped in the Cadillac and drove to Leicester where we knew some faces that Parko wanted to use for his shoot.

A few weeks later he called me and asked if I wanted to go with him to meet a guy he knew called Malcolm McLaren who Parko was working with on a new photo shoot. Malcolm was a real maverick, a nonconformist rebel with crazy, orange curly hair which he tried to tame into a greased back quiff. We knew he was trading old rockabilly vinyl records from a space at the back of Paradise Garage. So, the two of us headed down there to meet him. Malcolm told us he'd had an offer to take over the whole shop with his girlfriend Vivienne Westwood who was a schoolteacher. During that first meeting with Malc, he and I totally hit it off. He was fascinated by what I was up to and when I told him I had all this original rock and roll clothing and could source more from all over Britain, he loved the idea and so began an alliance. After that momentous afternoon, Parko and I were just standing on the King's Road, we had no fucking idea at the time of how this event would shape social history for the next forty years, but it did, and this was the exact moment that both Malcolm and I dived in and began our long and tortured journeys into the world of extraordinary people and alternative fashion..............

Off I went again, only this time driving around the streets of Liverpool and the coastal town of Weston-super-Mare, tracking down old ladies who were running their little village corner shops. The process would consist of me circling around the town searching out my prey which would generally be some old traditional style shop, a haberdashery or similar. It needed to be a sort of 'sell anything' type which most of them were back then. I would strut in acting like that dude with a blanket around his neck from the movie, A Few Dollars More, and I would survey the scene like a bank robber. I'd work out how to get behind the counter so I could rummage in the back rooms or upstairs where all the good stuff was kept. It wasn't that easy as they were scared shitless of this strangely dressed alien me! I found it helped if I banged a load of cash on the shop counter that usually got me into the all important redundant stock, which was exactly the gear I was after.

I loved driving around England causing mayhem and chaos, pulling up in my Cadillac, scaring the old folk. The truth is both me and McLaren were like pirates, as all the while I was working out how to get one over on the old lady so I could rifle through her stock, Malcolm was wringing his hands back in London like a modern-day Fagin singing ......you gotta pick a pocket or two. ....waiting for me to return to the smoke with my bag of swag.

On my return from these so called buying trips Malcolm would dive upside down into my Cadillac and go through the goods I'd pillaged, pulling out Rock Around the Clock shirts, Billy Fury flecked jackets and other iconic pieces. The next time I visited, Malcolm's shop looked fucking amazing. Larry Parnes, the impresario who from his office on Tin Pan Alley had managed several famous teen idols in the 50's and 60's would always be a major inspiration to Malcolm and he had replicated the famous photo of Tin Pan Alley from back in the 50's by placing old black Bakelite radios on the pavement outside. He had

taken down the old Paradise Garage sign and now massive hand painted, red letters read 'LET IT ROCK.' It was full of old vinyl records, vintage leather jackets, my 50's Rockabilly clothing, Rock'n'Roll debris, posters and memorabilia. On walking through the door, I was confronted by the guys from Kilburn and the High Roads, an early incarnation of The Blockheads, who were dressed head to foot in Teddy Boy outfits. There was a dwarf with her tits out, Malcolm was in an Edwardian jacket and hand painted tie and the juke box was all lit up playing Billy Fury really fucking loud! It was pure genius.

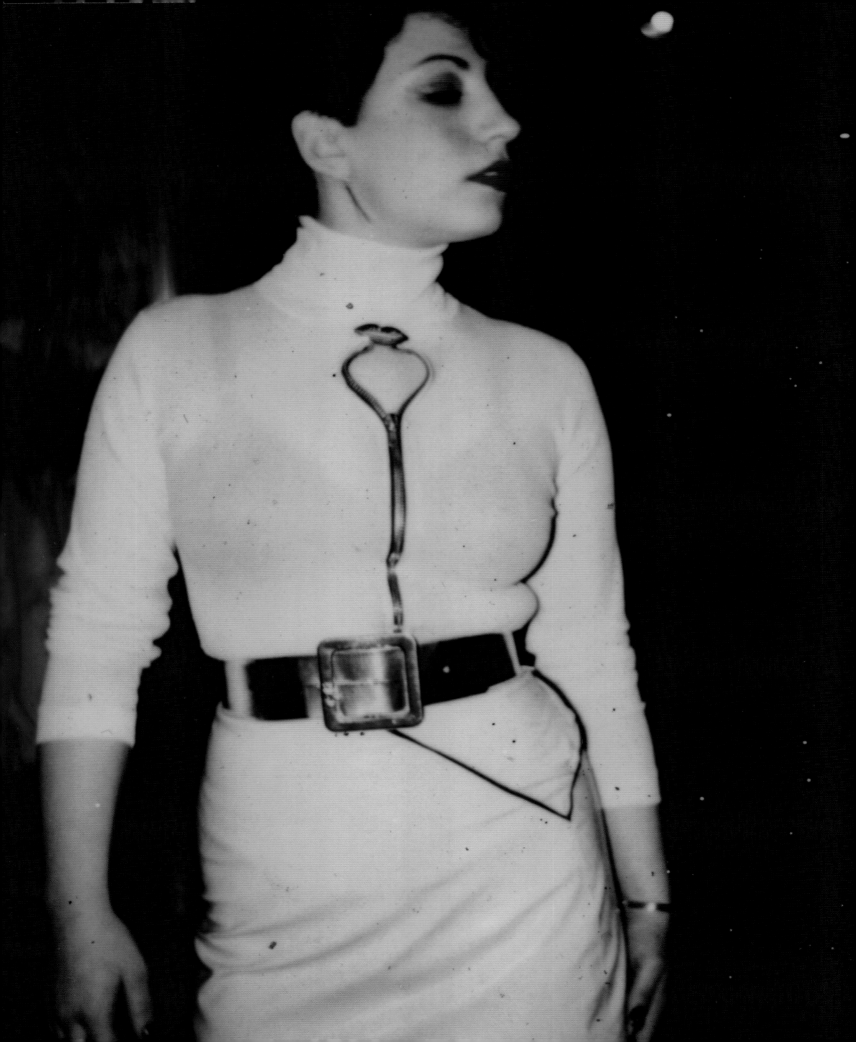

JK and the Mighty Don

I continued to drive back and forth regularly from Leicester to London as I was still supplying Malcolm with original 50's clothing. Everything was going great but I knew there was more. Sure, I didn't know what I wanted or how to get it, or if I would even recognise it if it happened, but I could sense something was in the air. On one particular day I took a walk up the King's Road to see what was going on when an old Renault screeched to a halt and out jumped this guy. Leaving the car door wide open he charged across the road and ran straight up to me, I thought he was going to fucking attack me. Instead he said he loved what I was wearing and wanted to know where I got my gear from and what I was doing there on the King's Road. I told him how I'd been supplying Malcolm's shop with clobber and he asked me if I could get hold of any more, of course I could, I had a tonne of the stuff.

John Krivine and I hit it off immediately. He said he wanted to take me for lunch to talk business and as I'd never met a geezer as posh as him in Leicester, or anywhere else for that matter, I was intrigued and agreed to go along. Turned out he was a public schoolboy and I later found out that he was also so much more. I knew this was going to be a real education for a northern twat like me, but I could also tell straight away that we had a lot of serious stuff in common and that I was going to like him. I assumed he'd take me to some fancy restaurant but no, he took me to a fish and chip shop in Brixton, South London. The first lesson I learned on meeting John was to expect the unexpected. The area was alien to me and might as well have been Africa. I thought I knew all about London from Soho to Chelsea, Portobello Road and the West End but I'd never been South before so this was an eye opener.

During lunch he asked about the clothes I was wearing, I was in a white flecked Billy Fury sports jacket, peg trousers and white winkle picker shoes. He then asked about Malcolm's shop and about what was happening on the King's Road, he seemed to be excited about the scene that was building up there. By the time we'd finished eating he'd made me an offer I couldn't refuse.

I didn't know if he was bullshitting or not, but I decided to go along with it anyway, so we agreed that I would source the clothes and he would deal with the business side of things beginning with locating some premises. I couldn't have made it up, it was everything I'd dreamed of and for me this meeting was my equivalent to the moment Brian Epstein discovered The Beatles.

JK immediately hooked me up with a free flat in the Oval so I moved on in. I didn't know where the fuck I was, it was still such an undiscovered part of London. I don't think it even featured on street maps it was so dodgy. I was made up though, it was a real stroke of good fortune bumping into him, things were on the up. A few days later I transported the rest of the stock down from Leicester in a van and so it all began.

John was a creative guy and already had a shop in Brixton dealing in vintage jukeboxes like the Bubble Wurlitzer. That was his main business and he had a customer list that included the likes of Led Zeppelin. I was fucking impressed as I'd been buying jukeboxes too but mine were more sci-fi machines like the Meteor which resembled Robby the Robot from the 1958 movie, Forbidden Planet. I'd been getting good bucks for my stuff but my edge, and John recognised it, was all the contacts I had. He had the chequebook and we could see that together we could ditch his shop in Brixton and move to a better part of town. We bombed around London looking at property and John was writing out cheques like there was no tomorrow, the only thing was that he went through the entire cheque book and every one of them bounced. I was thinking what the fuck is happening here, it felt like the dream had already turned to a nightmare. Next thing I knew we were called into an emergency meeting at his bank to discuss the matter. Now I had been to banks in Leicester and London, but I'd never been to a bank like this. It was Lloyds of London in the City and it was the size of the Pantheon in Rome. We were led into a panelled boardroom, we sat down, and I was waiting for the shit to hit the fan. Now here's the twist I hadn't seen coming, John's father was a major shareholder in the bank. The whole mess was sorted pretty fast and fucking hell, I realised I'd got me a get out of jail free card! I definitely slept well that night.

Later that week JK had already fixed us up with a unit and guess where? On the King's Road! This first space he found was in an antiques market called Antiquarius and being right smack in the middle of Chelsea it was next to all the antique dealers and their rich customers, so we set up shop and within a week we had completely sold out of all our stock. Fuck me, it seemed like every cool cat in town had found out we were there. We sold to hip hairdressers, photographers, the fashion set, street kids and magazine stylists, we sold to them all. We needed more stock so I needed to head back out fast. I was hitting up all my old haunts that I'd frequented when picking up supplies for McLaren. No one paid much rent back in those days, it was before capitalism and greed really set in, so most of these shops had piles of old shit they were happy to virtually give away and the idea of nostalgia or vintage didn't exist back then.

I arrived back in London with a van full of stuff and we crammed it all into a lock up but the space was far too small, so we went in search of something larger. We found a space in an old railway arch, somewhere around Bermondsey, and went ahead and rented it. Later, bands like The Damned, The Sex Pistols and Chelsea (early Generation X) used it as a rehearsal space. I remember stuff would always go missing after those rehearsals but that's another story.

We stocked up the stall again and things were really kicking off. By now there was a chick called Susie running it for us, she had a wonderful, kind of 60's shop girl vibe with sharp bobbed hair, bit arty, bit posh, which I liked coming from Leicester where girls like that didn't exist. She was perfect for Chelsea, the manor we were trading in. She was the girlfriend of Andy Czezowski our accountant at the time. Now we knew we were popular and could make the business a success so we decided it was time to move on up. We took a new space at Antiquarius which was twice the size. We noticed the unit next to ours was run by a guy called Bernie Rhodes, he was selling freshly made Hawaiian style shirts covered in American cars like Cadillacs. I couldn't really tell where that was going as

an idea but at that time he was just trying to find his way like we all were. Of course, later he would manage The Clash and we all know where that took him!

After a while Susie wanted to move on so we put the word out that we were after a new manager. Not long after we got a job application from a guy called Don Letts. Maybe it was meant to be or maybe it was an improbable relationship that may never otherwise have happened but it did and I'll never forget it. When me and Don first set eyes on each other there was a moment of edginess between us, a kind of power play. Nobody could have been more surprised than me to see this young black kid walk through the door. I wasn't sure if he would be the right person to take charge of my aesthetically cool, super-hot, fashionable store. I mean I just thought 'This ain't happening" but boy was I wrong.

Don wasn't like anyone I'd met before, he was a soul boy with an Afro and looked like he didn't give a shit. I really wasn't sure if he'd be right for us but he was very ambitious and he told me he could handle the whole thing. He was always a powerful guy, I could tell that from the moment we met. Sure, he had an Afro and had been working in a shitty jeans shop, but he had a good attitude, and he wanted to get on. He came through the job interview with flying colours and I could tell he would work really well for us and he wanted to move on up, so we offered him the position and he snapped at the chance. God knows why, as even we didn't know how our new enterprise was going to pan out long term. I still don't know what he saw in the two of us, me and John Krivine, but we grabbed him quickly and that was a great move as he had a gift I hadn't seen coming.

One evening he invited me over to his place and he showed me around. He'd collected some nice pieces of cool furniture as well as a very impressive record collection which included white music, bands like The Beatles and Hall and Oates but more importantly tons of Dub Reggae that he'd been importing from Jamaica which had never been heard in the UK before. He was a laugh to hang out with and always a smooth talker. So, I supplied the clothes, JK did the business and all the society mingling and Don managed the stall. We were the three Musketeers. Soon after a fourth person,

Jeannette Lee, who was a friend of Don's joined us. She was special, and she fascinated me, we would talk for hours about everything. With Jeannette on board the team was complete and what a fucking team we must've looked, me the Leicester twat, JK my posh Jewish business partner, Don the hip young black kid and our East End girl Jeannette. I was thinking this could just be crazy enough to work, we were tight together and it did have a flavour of New York about it. We called it Acme Attractions and it was about to become a legend.

We were in trouble though as the antique market had had enough of us by then. There were constantly crowds of soul boys queuing outside the market before it even opened, it was hilarious. These boys didn't give a fuck about antiques and would knock them over as they marched in and made their way to our stall. By luck though the basement was empty, no one wanted to trade down there so as a last resort it was offered to us. Fuck me it was brilliant, Don dragged his gigantic, fucking speakers down there and played his dub sounds full blast! With everything now set up in the previously unloved basement we could do whatever we wanted, sell whatever we wanted and play whatever we wanted. We had ourselves a Chelsea Boutique. It was the sharpest place to be. Of course, we didn't know if anyone would descend to the basement so we put the sign up at the top of the hallowed stairs with the legendary words ACME ATTRACTIONS. It's a name that still pricks up the ears of anyone who crossed over that line and ventured down to our Aladdin's cave.

They did come down those stairs, in their hundreds in fact and it became like a place of worship for the style kids of the day. Don was getting into his groove; his dub sounds were notorious with the white club kids and would influence a new generation that became the Punks. Me and Don would hang out after hours and get into bad boy stuff, it was almost like having our own nightclub and on any given day you could bump into the likes of Bob Marley looking for some weed or Chrissie Hynde or Burning Spear who just wanted a place to hang out. So, ACME became legend and has a place in history as where it all began.

I met up with Don recently and we talked about what went down over the years. For those of you who don't know, Don went on to be a member of Big Audio Dynamite, a DJ and filmmaker and Jeannette a member of P.I.L as well as MD of Rough Trade. Don is quoted as saying, "subcultures formed in the U.K. because the mainstream was not satisfying the needs of certain people like myself. So, through music and through style, we found our tribe, we found like-minded rebels". He told me at that meeting that the Acme days were some of the best of his life and that none of those subcultures would have ever happened back then if it wasn't for me putting the whole Acme scene together, I replied, "Don, let me tell you, we both took it to the bank".

Living on the front line

I was approached by a guy who'd had dealings with Malcolm McLaren, but Malcolm had given him a couple of rubber cheques, so he wasn't too happy. Anyway, he asked if I would be interested in some suits made by original old London tailors. Of course, I jumped at the chance, so off we went, a bit like the wily old fox and Pinocchio but on the back streets of London's East End, gangster land of the Krays.

Back at the tailors, we entered a scruffy old building and going up the stairs it looked like a page out of a Dickens novel. Then up yet more stairs until we opened a door into another world. We might as well have just stepped into the Tardis and gone back about a hundred years. We asked the governor there if he could make us some 1950's style suits and peg trousers in a range of colours including electric blue and bright pink. Bob's your uncle, Fanny's your aunt. These guys didn't need any more direction, they'd made this kind of gear a million times before. We went back to Chelsea and waited on our first delivery. The suits arrived and were as sweet as a nut. We couldn't keep up with the demand, these suits and strides marched straight out the door, we sold every single piece in that first weekend.

We realised we were going to need an office and work space as demand was really growing. Portobello was another part of London I loved that like the King's Road was also famous in the 60's. It was where I'd started out with my first stall a few years back. It was an edgy area where Rastas in red, gold and green with their really fucking loud speakers were pumping out reggae. We were offered a building right on the Portobello Road so we took that. This was the perfect place for us to position our hardcore creative offices and it had a small shop downstairs which we called Acme Surplus. We began designing our own stuff starting out with a few T-shirts. A young guy called Philip Sallon pitched up, he could tell we had a cool vibe going at Acme and he fancied himself as a designer. So he joined us and we started making our own shit in the work room upstairs.

Back then we called our office the 'front line'. Sallon would be on the sewing machine, making the tea or prancing around the workshop in big Y fronts, he looked about 17 at the time, perhaps he was. We worked on various zipped items, like black T-shirts that were covered in metal zips sewn on at obtuse angles. We also made T-shirts with tyre prints over them. I came up with the idea of how to make them – I used to park my huge Yankee Chevy up on the pavement, right outside Surplus and I decided I would just ink up the tyres and drive up and down the Portobello Road over the T-shirts. Kind of hit and run style. Everything was so free and easy back then.

We were always talking about music, we knew the scene well and we sensed we could develop a band, back then that was the thing to be into. We didn't know anything about how to pull a band together though so we put an ad in Melody Maker for musicians. Gene October, a singer, had been hanging around for a while with Sheila Rock and Janet Street Porter in tow and we were looking for musicians to join him. One day there was a knock on the door and a young Billy Idol was standing out on the pavement. He was 21 but he looked about 18, good-looking and extremely polite. He didn't look like Billy Idol back then, he had dark hair and was well spoken with an air of confidence which was charming and an aura that made him special. Anyway, we were upstairs making our black, metal zip t's at the time so he just mucked in up there on odd days and started hanging out at our ACME store on The King's Road. Billy had so much energy and he was determined to make things happen. I knew this kid was going to do something different. Gene and Billy along with Tony James and John Tower ended up forming the band Chelsea under our management. We let them practice in our railway arch in the arse end of South East London.

Ready steady go

I'd arranged a gig at The Chelsea Potters, the most famous pub on the King's Road, which was one block from Acme. We were putting Billy Idol on stage for the first time with the rest of the band, Gene October was the front man at the time though as it was still the Chelsea line up. The Bromley contingent also turned up with Siouxsie and some of the Banshees who had come to offer their support to Billy. I'd taken some of my Acme boys along and told them that this was my new venture and they'd said they wanted to come down to see what was going on. Well they fucking hated it. They all started laughing saying that everyone looked like a bunch of fucking wankers and that the crowd jumping up and down were prats, the kids in the crowd were doing the pogo. That fucking sealed it for me and I knew Acme was over. Later on, I remember our accountant Andy nicking the band Chelsea from us. Quickly though I could tell that managing a band wasn't going to be my cup of tea if you know what I mean. Gene October and

Billy were getting too much and I knew Idol was heading for bigger things. After a few gigs Billy, Tony and John split from Gene and the band Generation X emerged. One day he played me a song he'd just written called Ready Steady Go, of course I fucking loved it. I was proud to play my part in mentoring Billy and helping to finance his band. Andy seemed to get his head around everything we were doing from then on and went off to open The Roxy. Not the most ingenious name in the world but hey who cares.

Towards the end of Acme, I went back and grabbed my old girlfriend Helen and brought her down from Leicester to the smoke with me. I don't know why after all I was finished with Leicester, maybe I felt guilty about how it had ended or something or maybe I thought we'd still got a chance. She was talented, she could assist me and she looked great so she moved to the Oval with me and we tried living together.

I was always pushing my girlfriends into the headlines. It's just something I did. In the past ex-girlfriends have asked why I did that, I didn't care back then, but recently I get mad when I see that they've taken all the credit for everything I'd done but yeah, I guess if they were going to be by my side I wanted people to know who they were and why I'd chosen to be with them as my partner in crime. I'd get a thrill when I gave a girl the key to my life and the combination to my safe, she would then have all the power over me to dish the dirt, enough to put me away and take everything.

So, Helen and I were together for a while, then I moved to the King's Road and rented a bedsitter with a shoe designer mate, Helen wasn't around for a while but I don't remember why. Anyway, I was living close to Acme and that was great fun. I would take all the dosh back there every night and we were really raking it in, in fact I'd never seen so much money. I'd throw it on the carpet then roll around in it and laugh just like in the film 'The Knack and How to Get It'! At this point I had to make a decision, Punk was on the lips of the chosen few. Philip Sallon was hanging around with the Bromley contingent including Billy Idol of course, all the signs were there to make a move. We were on the verge of Punk. Don didn't like the idea of shifting onto Punk though and got a shock when he came into Acme one morning to find I'd been up all night and turned it into a Punk shop. I mean yeah, it was a tough decision but as you read my story you'll see I've had to make loads of tough decisions…. But when someone is waving a big fucking flag at me saying come and get it I had to jump ship. I can't deny that the thrill is always there, some people get their kicks from champagne, some from heroin, some from sport and some from having kids and buying a fucking washing machine. I just loved diving into the abyss, do or die, crash and burn, what else is there to do?

BOY

153 KING'S ROAD LONDON SW3

THE STRENGTH OF THE COUNTRY LIES IN ITS YOUTH

PART OF THE ACME ATTRACTIONS ORGANISATION

153 King's Road

It was time to move on and up our game again. We were ready to leave the basement and get out on the main thoroughfare. We knew we didn't want to be at the cheaper end of the street where Malcolm's place, now renamed SEX was, so we took a big risk and rented the unit at 153 King's Road. We wanted to change everything, the style, the clothes, the customers, everything, including the name. There are plenty of idiotic people that think it must have been easy to create the brand BOY. One person said to me recently "Big deal, wow, you took a T-shirt and scribbled BOY on it". That's not how it happened at all and in reality, coming up with a simple name that really works and grabs people's attention, like say The Smiths or The Who, is actually genius. Shops at the time had names like Jean Junction, Emperor of Wyoming, Great Gear Market, Fortnum and Mason, Butler and Wilson. There was no fucking Gap or Next or FCUK. BOY created a template for future retailing.

Anyway, JK and I had a number of meetings with these two young artists, the reason for the meetings was to discuss the concept and name for the new King's Road premises. These two artists had taken inspiration from Wild Boys, by William S. Burroughs which later inspired the iconic T-shirt Cigarette Boy. These artists had been collecting newspaper cuttings and headlines referencing dead boys, most notably headlines like 'Boy stabs PC' and 'Boy electrocuted at 30,000 vaults'. We decided we wanted to frame some of the cuttings and stick them up around the shop. Then we had the idea to turn the whole thing into a kind of art piece. As a concept it was pretty involved and revolutionary and took plenty of what we now call brainstorming for us to arrive at the simple but inspired name BOY.

So it was decided, BOY would be the name of the shop and huge brutalist metal letters that spelt out the word BOY were made to hang outside. The shop was blacked out and we lay down black rubber flooring. Medical cabinets were assembled and hung on big chrome chains in the window. The finishing touches were the Doc Marten boots which had just arrived and the framed artworks with pictures of the dead bodies

of electrocuted boys. I decided to use 9-inch nails to attach the Doc Marten boots to the walls. The idea was to create a scenario where a boy had died in a fire in the shop. To make it look real I actually set fire to the fuckin walls then put what looked like dismembered remains of the boy's body in the medical cabinets in the window. A little old lady walked up to the window, peered in, screamed then fucking collapsed. That was the moment the police arrived and took me away. Job done.

Of course we're talking about the 70's here. A time when there were no mobile phones, only stinking red phone boxes, no internet, not even fax machines. Just handmade flyers stuck to the walls of the dark, dank streets of London telling the cool kids where to go to get their kicks. It might as well have been the dark ages when it came to technology, communication and marketing but somehow, via nothing more than word of mouth the fame of this notorious act spread fast, far and wide.

When we finally launched people couldn't understand why we called it BOY, they actually asked me why we'd chosen it, they said it would never work, that it was stupid and didn't mean anything. It was just a generic word, boy. What the fuck did they know? I knew we'd hit on something though the moment I saw how the huge metal letters outside were intimidating the civvies as they passed by. It felt like the birth of Christ, the adoration of the BOY. The chance for young boys and girls to wear whatever the fuck they wanted. It was a symbol of the new youth culture. It was fucking great and it changed things forever.

Pop music had stopped progressing, so street kids started creating their own scenes and they came piling into BOY. We were offering something that wasn't available anywhere else. They flocked in everyday, totally disinterested in any political shit or unrest that was going on. As it happens they were about to join in, although at that point they didn't know it. What they did know was that they were beginning to make the establishment uneasy. They were having some kind of effect on society and their disapproval rating with the public was going up. They were becoming the "young Punks", and they were headline news. Suddenly the youth were on the march….. It was a time of social unrest in the UK.

In those early days BOY was full of fucking Punks, angry and lost, wearing DIY Punk clothing. Bin bags were the haute couture of the day, and safety pins, LOADS of safety pins. Spiked hair, bondage shorts, bondage trousers, Clash pants, muslin tops and zip T-shirts. We had Malcolm's Sex Pistols blaring out at full blast. Sid Vicious came in one day wearing high heels. The shop window was always being kicked in by football hooligans, the old teddy Boys and right-wing Skinheads. The Church even had a go at us by chucking red paint at the window because we had the Madonna and child as a display! Tourists were too scared to visit BOY in case they got gobbed on! The Punk movement was spreading rapidly across the country.

The British Punk scene was different from the American scene of a few years earlier. Over a decade earlier The Beatles had copied the American Rock and Roll artists like Chuck Berry and Elvis and created a massive teenage pop scene, starting in Britain it was unrivalled anywhere in the world. This time the British Punks were kicking down the doors of the establishment and parading like peacocks up and down the King's Road and hanging around outside BOY under its slogan "The strength of the country lies in its youth". For years afterwards the front of BOY became the posing spot where Punks from around the world wanted to be photographed.

Photographs were and are big part of our scene, I'm glad because we captured a moment in time. One trick we had up our sleeves involved photographing the goings on in the shop changing rooms, customers and celebrities alike. There was one girl with her own TV show that was a regular visitor to the shop and enjoyed having sex with the young Punks in those changing rooms…. the next day the pictures were put in the window and along came Mr. Plod the policeman to cart me away again.

Most shops come and go, just taking up space on the high street, and then there are the shops you remember; the local fish and chip shop, the record shop, the guitar shop, the hairdresser's and the greasy spoon café. There are very few that actually changed everything and turned the world upside down, a revolution. We turned BOY into an experience, a place where kids went to get away from home, a space that spoke to them, where they could express themselves, a hedonistic mind fuck, a space and time to meet others, compete with them, dress like them, the kids that could hardly wait for the weekend so they could be back there, be who they really wanted to be.

This was BOY and once you stepped through the door you were transported into another world, you became part of the In Crowd. We created a kind of sacred atmosphere, likened to a church, a religion. A movement so strong you could feel the presence of some other power. The power of thousands of visitors, customers, pilgrims, devotees and loyal fans.

Youth was on the march; the old days of Harold Wilson had gone and Callaghan was in. Shows like The Old Grey Whistle Test were OK, but they were slow to recognise Punk.

During my entire history I seem to have also created events and movements when opening my shops. I never like to think of them as shops, they were places for kids to hang out, meeting places for the marginalised. More like the installations, pop-ups or event spaces that we're used to today. To me, this was the most exciting sector of our society. It was always like that, I was thinking 20 years ahead and you can see the influence of BOY in every part of youth fashion and culture from clubbing to streetwear, gay and bi. It was about individual sexual freedom years before it hit the mainstream marketplace and long before it turned up in the provinces.

Rants, Raves and Revolutions

Let's rewind for a second and take a look back at how I got here and what was driving me this far, motivating me, screwing me up, pinning me down, angering me. For this book is about me and all I gained and learned about everything, not just fashion or running a business but about relationships, deceit, commitment, people and everything else. So, let's start there, I don't like ordinary people, but I do like amazing people, I don't mean successful but I do mean imaginative creatives, those that are reaching out hungry for something, perhaps just the right word or look, I know a lot of people like that.

Let's face it, it's difficult for me to know what's going on, I'm just following where life takes me or whoever the latest person is that's taking me there. I've never been religious but something bigger than me guides me and considering my school gave up on me and my home town would have left me for dead, I have no idea how any of this has happened, but things keep on happening to me and I still don't know why, so fuck knows what you'll make of it all. Anyway, enough about psychology for the moment let's take a look at my world as this could be the perfect moment to reflect on the journey so far and what's actually going through my head as I'm writing.

Not me
(Rants, Raves and Revolutions)

They say bands like The Fall, The Smiths, New Order and The Buzzcocks are some of the best, the most brilliant in the world in fact, well I agree and I've seen Talking Heads, Johnny Thunders and Zappa and it's all fucking great but I'm British, and there's something that runs through your blood when you listen to Fun Boy Three, Smiley Culture, The Streets, A Certain Ratio, 808 State, Blur or Pulp. It's everything, It's everywhere. They say it's the weather – British kids had nothing better to do but practice in a garage somewhere, and so the British band culture was born. I went to see The Pistols at their first gig and I noticed the roadies looked like the original road crew for the Small Faces. There were loads of amps behind the band and they actually opened up with a cover of "What You Gonna Do About It" by The Small Faces, from that moment I just knew how big they were going to become. Malcolm had visions of them being the next Bay City Rollers but he seriously miscalculated the whole thing, they were actually so much better than he had predicted. It was pure raw power and it blew me away!

I've been dragged up through the most important age possible, from Bohemians to British Soul, Prog Rock, Glam, Punk and all the rest so it was hard to sit still and that's why I couldn't stay with one look, one style, one movement. For me, it felt like it was all one thing but it changed so fast. I didn't like the industry, as soon as I had created a look, a movement, it was time to leave it behind. I was always obsessed by what was coming next, but the raw, early work I did was always the best.

There was a constant fight in my head, I'd be thinking how great it would be if I could get perfect clothes made, but then that meant dealing with factory ideology. Those guys not only wanted big orders but they were always fucking copying me so everything ended up losing its originality. The best look, before Punk hit and everything was copied, was in the Acme days of East End tailored peg trousers, plastic sandals, homemade T-shirts and string mohair jumpers.

My culture clash was to exist as a creator, but not like those French and Italian designers; they knew nothing about the British streets or the music that cut through our veins. Life felt so suicidal, so urgent, so high………
……I felt all of these emotions when creating.

Sitting in a design office – that's like doing time, like being locked up. I could get more stimulation from the Silver Street pub on darts night, with pie and peas or a cheese and beetroot cob.

Not to mention the buzz of driving my Cortina through the streets of Sheffield on a Saturday night, eating faggot, chips and mushy peas, or curry and chips from Ali's chip shop in Leicester! His shop was in the papers for having dead dogs in a bath out the back, but we still went there.

My life was my work, so I couldn't let either be boring. That's why BOY became so much more than a fashion label; much, much more. It became something to believe in, and people could sense that there was something going on. It had nothing to do with fashion………. it was beyond fashion.

Destroy

This is the BOY story behind the Destroy T-shirt. The image of Johnny Rotten of the Sex Pistols along with the song Anarchy in the UK made this T-shirt one of the most desirable pieces of British Punk clothing ever made. Punk devotees and enthusiasts are often confused to see the BOY label on some of these T-shirts. They assume they must be fakes but nothing could be further from the truth because back in the very early and infamous days of Punk there were two important shops that opened on the King's Road in Chelsea.

The King's Road was given its famous name because it was the road that King Charles II and his entourage would travel along on their way to his palace at Kew. Fast forward to the 1960's and the King's Road was in the headlines once more when it played host to Mary Quant, Granny Takes a Trip and the Chelsea Drug Store and so marked the start of the Swinging 60's. This was one of the most iconic periods on the King's Road for fashion, music and movies. It was frequented by The Small Faces, The Kinks and The Rolling Stones and later Pink Floyd and Led Zeppelin. It was soon to become one of the most famous streets not only in England's green and pleasant land but also around the world.

That was because a bunch of upstarts, anarchists and undesirables decided to invade in the mid 70's, making it their own and according to local residents bring filth and depravity with them! Of course, the press loved this kind of shit and it was often the newspapers at the time that came up with the titles like 'the Swinging 60's' and 'Punk Rock'. Who gives a fuck anyway, all I know is we'd arrived and we were breaking down doors and scaring the establishment.

It was 1976 and Seditionaries had taken over from SEX and I opened BOY. We immediately had everyone in the street talking about us, at that point in time all the other places were jeans joints like the Jean Machine which was still hanging in there after their heydays in the 60's. It was time for change, in fact it was a change of direction so definitive that it would alter the course of social history once again. Malcolm of course opened

way down at the poor end of the road, known as World's End, where Hippies still congregated wearing afghan coats who would spit on us. They really hated us which we thought was great and it confirmed to me that I was right to leave the Hippie shit behind.

When the BOY shop opened it was bang in the middle of the King's Road, a prime location from which we would use the shop to cause as much trouble and destruction as possible and we did. Teddy Boys hated us, yes those fuckers again, I thought I'd seen the last of them back on Brighton beach in the 60's when as Mods we kicked the shit out of them. The football hooligans were just as bad, they would kick our front windows in just for kicks. The Punks however loved us and turned up at BOY in their marauding hordes asking for the Destroy shirt. They hit upon our shop first so we would have to send them all the way down the road to Seditionaries. In the end the demand was so great that there was a discussion about doing a deal so that the shirt could sell in both places, we also set up a license for me to manufacture them, so don't worry, if you've got one with a BOY label then its prob legit. Funny thing is 40 odd years later both versions of the shirt are worth loads of money, if only I still had a few of the fuckers…

Following on from that BOY was offered all the McLaren/Westwood Punk print designs. It became apparent that there was potentially great business to be had by continuing to sell the original, classic Punk T-shirts to the hundreds of Punk kids up and down the country. From BOY's perspective it was an excellent way to join forces and create one of the first ever collaborations of street fashion. Not only would it satisfy the eager young Punks desperate to own one of these iconic shirts but would also keep the artistry of the designs alive and allow the collection to flourish. So we started to produce the Destroy T-shirt along with other iconic prints including Vive Le Rock, Mickey and Minnie, Snow White, Punk Hell, Tits and Smoking Boy. I was more than happy to add them to my arsenal of BOY designs. I had always felt that these prints were a form of art and I was also interested in new ideas and concepts for the way in which art could be sold. We were doing great business and the collaboration was going great, however there was one fly in the ointment, which was the famous case of the Mickey and Minnie T-shirt. Seemingly, it didn't go down that well with the lawyers at Disney that we were using the images without permission…. This resulted in a bloody lawsuit being bought against BOY. We lost the case and Disney were awarded £40,000 in costs. Well I guess the image did portray Mickey and Minnie fucking……. ha ha!

There was a young anarchist artist called Jamie Reid who was an important part of the scene. He was the Enfant Terrible of Punk art and he became famous for the work he produced for The Sex Pistols, which are some the most recognisable and important images from the Punk era. I really liked him and decided that I would put on an entire exhibition of his work at BOY. We featured T-shirts and posters from his 'Up They Rise' collection including the famous Fuck Forever print. His work is still very sought after and fortunately for me this time I've held on to a few of his pieces I exhibited. You lose some, you win some….

GOD Save

RONNIE BiGGS

Punk
(Rants, Raves and Revolutions)

Punk was a quick blast, but I guess that was the beauty of it. It was never meant to last, and although it was as fast as it's three-minute songs, the legend and legacy of Punk is still relevant today. So, I suppose with the addition of bands that were arguably Punk or New Wave like The Jam and The Stranglers, or Pop Punk like the Buzzcocks, then if you count the beginning in New York with the Ramones and the Stooges which happened a couple of years earlier, it probably lasted as long as any other cult movement. There's no doubt though that it's legacy is ongoing and still causing controversy. I remember discussing it with Don Letts once for some project he was working on...... we came up with loads of optional thinking, but to nail it as far as UK Punk is concerned the eye of the storm was about 2 years. Bands like The Clash turned it into a full-time job,

along with others like Billy Idol who started out working for me in the BOY shop in the King's Road where I put together his first band, Chelsea – just before Generation X. I guess you could say the Punk movement and the fallout probably lasted as long as the Hippie movement did, whatever, after 2 years I'd had enough of Punk and I was getting really bored.

To sum it up, Punk was an explosion, a movement of huge significance, and these moments of British music and culture, art, fashion and subculture are the glue that binds Britain's youth together. Whether it was the Beatniks, Teddy Boys, Hippies, Football Hooligans, Mods and Rockers rioting on the beaches, Punks, Romantics, Goths, Ravers or club culture – I WAS THERE and BOY was an amalgamation of it all....

SEDITIONARIES

Vivienne Westwood 1976

TSHIRT
Top quality American cotton T Shirt.
Black, white or red
£5.50 incl. p. & p.

MUSLIN
Double layer, cheese cloth.
D rings, dog clips.
Black or white.
£9.50 incl. p. & p.

God Save

Anarchy

Cowboys

Call
01 - 351 1115

FOR
DETAILS
ABOUT
THIS
PRINT

CENSORED

Your mother

Mickey & Minnie

Wake Up

Destroy

Punk Gang

Vive le Rock

Snow White

Prick up your ears

Marilyn

PX Covent Garden

Anyway, I got bored with plastic bin liners and safety pins pretty quickly and I made a mental plan about my life, a plan that I must never ever let things get boring. Sure, we were having a great time, Don Letts and I would go down the Roxy to watch the bands. We saw them all, Generation X of course, Siouxsie and the Banshees and The Clash, who Don would go on to direct loads of music videos for. The Punk vibe was everywhere. I remember making a boiler suit for Mark P from Sniffin' Glue, all the Punk bands were hanging out, The Pistols, The Damned, X-Ray Spex. Life was sweet, life was good but the excitement for me was putting it all together and watching what happened. I was creating and I loved it, I realised many years later this was what I got off on and I was ready to go again.

It was 1978 and I had a feeling I could open up the wastelands of Covent Garden. Formerly a famous flower market that had recently closed down and moved out to the wilds of Vauxhall, South London. I found a market lock up shop with offices above for a pretty low rent. It appealed to me as I could live upstairs and start work immediately on the space downstairs. It was weird never seeing anyone, the area was completely deserted, we were alone, but it was perfect for us and also exciting to be in those dark, empty streets. I took the very first shop in the entire market on James Street. I was really motivated to start this new venture as once again I'd found a weird part of London, empty and desolate. Rats were cockily running around the streets in the piles of rubbish left by striking dustmen, yet the majestic Royal Opera House stood right opposite. There were the now empty old market pubs with 24 hour opening times and Covent Garden underground station which was hardly ever working and when it was no one used it anyway. It was as if everything was still in black and white.

I had ideas and a concept for the new shop that had never been seen before. The aim was to create a low tech, industrial installation and an inside-out interior. I'd recently been walking around the wonderland of Paris and seeing the industrial architecture of buildings such as Les Halle's and the Centre Pompidou. Also, the interiors of clothing stores by designers like Thierry Mugler and Jean Paul Gaultier.

I decided to keep the original metal, lock up shutter as the exterior door; all the pipes were left visible and there was exterior tubing running right through the shop interior. At the very back was a giant industrial clock which signified Flash Gordon, Kraftwerk, George Orwell's 1984's big brother and the factory worker. There were metal cages to display the clothes and industrial lighting, the rumour was that we nicked it all from the old MI5 building on Curzon Street which was closing down. I think I'll keep quiet about that one......... I called it PX after the army surplus provision stores which sold everything from Coca Cola to cameras, boots and clothing. The idea was to create the effect of a metal shelved store room on an army base and the final touch was the light box PX sign and metal TV spy monitor that we put up outside to announce our arrival.

Inside PX the clothing collection was well thought out and unique. I'd travelled to Amsterdam, Brussels and Paris to source objects of apparel that were different and unexpected. There were Flash Gordon tops with electro flashes resembling lightning bolts and studded shirts with diagonal piping with strict electro styling. We sold Peg trousers in pleated leather or with piping down the side to create a military feel as well as black leather jeans. There were long black leather coats and original grey German submarine jackets. On the back wall were suit jackets and trousers, the jackets had velvet shawl collars and we teamed them up with shirts in deep colours, vintage brooches, medals, sashes, leather hats and huge Kodak bags. To add to the surrealism of it all Steve Strange, with his big quiff and distinctive look was employed as the manager and not long after he was joined by the new shop girl, the alluring Princess Julia to whom I would become very close.

I travelled back up to a factory I knew in Leicester to get my Robin of Sherwood designs made up in leather and suede. There were the now famous, classic frilly white PX shirts, pirate pantaloons and buccaneer shirts. The press called it The New Romantics movement, Steve Strange was never happy about that, he always called it the Cult with No Name, but whatever the name, the style had shape shifted the look of the time and had become the essential wardrobe of every New Romantic band like Spandau Ballet, Steve Strange's Visage and a young Marilyn.

It was still so quiet around Covent Garden, there were no people, no shops, no cars, nothing. If we ever heard the sound of the lift at Covent Garden Station we knew around the corner would come a posse of flamboyant looking Romantics heading to PX. Every fucker who was anyone came through those doors………

From the hub of PX we literally ruled the New Romantics and became the name on the lips of everybody who was associated with the movement. Once again, the shop and its latest collections were ahead of the game as this was still the late 70's. Vivienne Westwood, who by this time had renamed her store Seditionaries, has said that she dubbed the New Romantic era to be between 1981 to 1985 but we were doing the look back in 78/79, way before it hit the wrong end of the King's Road. It's interesting how legend has been re-written. It was all about PX which was THE romantic store, right in the heart of a deserted Covent Garden.

I watched the area grow from 1978 to 1982, the golden years of the New Romantics and I'd found myself at the helm of another youth movement. Steve Strange was soon to explode onto the music scene as a bright star in the same way Billy had in the Acme/ BOY days.

I never told anyone the meaning of the name PX, for some reason my girlfriend at the time later claimed credit for the whole thing although she never even knew where the name came from.

The whole of Covent Garden was booming by now, the dark gas lit street feel had disappeared and been taken over by colourful places like the Dance Centre, the Sanctuary and Paul Smith. I remember the first major bar to open was called Rumours; we did promo T-shirts for the opening. It was a big bar and was full at the weekends with the new style crowd wearing GI outfits with padded shoulders and fox furs, most of them came from Canvey Island's famous Goldmine. Steve and his mate Rusty Eagan were running The Blitz club in a shabby old wine bar close by and it became the legendary home of the New Romantics. The Blitz club spawned bands like Spandau Ballet who played their first ever gig there, Depeche Mode, Soft Cell, Human League, Duran Duran and a young George O' Dowd, more of him later. They were dressed in loads of PX gear like our leather breaches and white, frilly shirts; we were part of the fashionista and music elite. The Blitz club door policy was absolute……. you could only get in if you were a New Romantic, it made it all the more elitist. Steve had learned that trick by coming to Le Palace club in Paris with me. People would turn up in the queue outside waiting to get in and hoping to meet Steve on the door. I remember one designer arriving wearing his best fringed bondage outfit. He should have known that no one was EVER going to get past Steve Strange wearing Westwood!

Steve had started Visage while he was working at PX with me Helen and Julia. I remember one day, just before his huge international hit Fade to Grey, Julia had come in complaining about the filming of the Fade to Grey video which she starred in. She relayed how she'd been strapped into a revolving chair and in her words, "It kept going round and round until I got fucking dizzy!" She didn't speak the French part in the video, as she's got such a strong cockney accent it would have been impossible for her to pull it off but she became famous for it anyway. That video along with Bowies' Ashes to Ashes, epitomised the era. Bowie of course was a huge influence on us all but Mick Jagger was famously turned away from The Blitz club for looking too old and boring, when he tried to blag his way in past Mr Strange.

A boy in Paris

The first time I met Paris was around 1976 and she was perhaps more exciting and beautiful than I had ever imagined, I was hooked. I call Paris 'she', because as a city Paris feels feminine. I was dragged up on the streets of Leicester, a city a long way from Paris especially back then. Everything in my hometown looked the same as it had at the end of World War Two. Even right up to the 70s England looked the same with gas street lamps, back-to-back Victorian houses, squalid conditions, outside toilets, no central heating and a tin bath that would hang on the wall outside to be brought in for Friday night bath time.

On moving to London and going through the biggest music and teen fashion movement ever, I had been enjoying a slightly more civilised view of life although still surrounded by city gents in bowler hats, pinstripe suits and leather briefcases. It wasn't my world, it was a type of old world order and felt really obsolete. Travel offered new experiences and cultures and a way to escape London and see the world through different eyes. I've always driven everywhere, it's without doubt my favourite travel experience. Anyway, back then telephone calls abroad were expensive and unreliable and there were no decent communication systems, so being a young entrepreneur, I preferred to drive around to get shit done, it was great. The M1 motorway had only been opened for a while and it had already made driving around from place to place a lot easier and back then there were fewer cars on the road. Even though the motorway system was still very basic it was better than it is now.

On the top of my list at the time was my desire to be the first of the young set to involve myself in Paris which was at the centre of the fashion houses and runway shows back then. There was a certain ambience on the streets of Paris that didn't exist in England. It was the centre of cafe culture and there was nothing like that going on in jolly old Blighty. I was fully aware that what I had been setting up in London was almost the complete opposite of Paris, with British Soul Boys, dub sounds and early bands playing the pub circuit. I wanted my share of both worlds though and it would become even more important to me that I had to create an international edge to what I was doing especially as at that time there were very few big fashion events in the UK. The London fashion council was struggling to find suitable venues and many designers couldn't be bothered to show there. Don't get me wrong, like McLaren, I was hooked on Svengalis and what Paris had that London didn't and vice versa, it was our little secret and he and I would use it to our advantage and strength. To be honest I loved it back then much more than I do now in the pure sense that back then we would create chaos and nobody knew what the fuck we were doing or how we were doing it.

Driving towards Paris, winter, spring or summer it didn't matter, it was just my desire to be in Paris, to die in Paris to crash and burn. I had to live it all. The first time I saw Paris it was 'burning'. Paris was like that and much more, driving in eight lanes of traffic with cars, motorbikes and taxis all weaving in and out playing with you. Driving under Charles de Gaulle airport under the fucking runway with planes taking off in front of you was enough to give you a heart attack. It was all part of the design, the city's design. Paris was like a woman but Britain was all male, and stiff upper lipped. She was sexual and all about theatre.

I'd go to the Bois de Boulogne by night where there were hundreds of beautiful trannies from all over the world and especially from Rio. Cars would queue up and the occupants would have conversations with the girls as they came out from behind the trees into the open and would crouch down next to the car to size up the driver. It was about L'amour but in a very special French way. Guys would get out of their cars and fuck trannies leaning against the trees, screaming harder, harder as a crowd would gather to watch the sport. It was the same all over Paris by night, it was a city whose spectacle and essence I could never get enough of. It was a million miles away from conservative London, it was haunting. Later I would take girls there for a ménage a trois if they were interested.

Around three or four in the morning I would hang around the area of Paris by the Moulin Rouge. I would order oysters and watch the French men that looked like Alain Delon with their small brimmed hats, perched at an angle on their heads smoking Gitanes and playing the Flipper Pin Ball machines. During the day I would go to a popular café for breakfast where there were so many different characters that I would just sit and people watch. The young garcons in waistcoats and white shirts would be laying lunch tables, a bearded guy would be reading a book in the corner, two women were ordering petit dejeuner, a girl and her dog would be taking 'café', just like a painting by Toulouse Lautrec. France was a place that totally fucking inspired me, I could design there. I would go to some of my favourite shops Upla, Hemisphere and Globe, I was younger than some of these designers and they had a different style to anything that was going on in London but there was an air of art colliding with fashion that filled me with pleasure. I would watch as the city began to show off its new Avant-Garde of emerging designers such as Gaultier, Kenzo, Agnes B and Mugler and I wanted to be a part of all of it.

'One day I went into the King's Road store and in the rear the wall looked like it had been decorated by being blasted with a flame thrower. I thought this was just genius.'

Chris Stein - Blondie

1980s

Endell St

Just before 1980 kicked in we had reached a point where we needed to start our own machine sewing room and that's when I decided it was time to move to a bigger site, plus Covent Garden St James Street was getting a bit too commercial. So, I found an entire four story building on Endell Street and I called it PX2. My formula for this shop was the complete opposite of PX1. Gone was the industrial, techno post Punk look and in came the sentimental look of deep stained wood and brass.

I wanted a Regency style interior that was lush almost museum like, with giant wood and glass cabinets which stood tall in the middle of the shop floor. I was nervous that customers wouldn't find us at this new address on the very edge of Covent Garden, but we were lucky again as in no time at all other shops started opening up around us. The whole area was going nuts. In the next street to us, Food for Thought, a vegetarian food emporium had just opened and was developing into a major business. On the corner of our street was a famous chippy, I'm pretty sure it was called something like Rock and Sole and next door there was a very popular jewellery store. There was a public house a couple of buildings along and Julia and I would start our drinking sessions in there. We became like Victorian drunks and she gave me everything, her time, attention and company day and night. We were really tight back then, roaming the gas lit streets of old London at night getting drunker and drunker.

She was perfect for this deception with her long hair tousled up and wearing a white Victorian dress, she really looked the part. I would be dressed in a Victorian school teachers suit with a bow tie, she wanted me like that. We were now the darlings of the press and New York's Fifth Avenue stores had got wind of our fame.

Buyers from Bloomingdales came by in a stretch limo and bought the entire contents of the shop explaining that they were going to put all our collections in their windows on Fifth Ave in order to tell the entire Romantic story. The shop lay empty and bare after Bloomingdales had plundered it like pirates leaving nothing but empty hangers! Funny thing is, as the buyers finished loading the bags into the stretch limo I over-heard them saying "oh my god, we've never bought stock in bin liners before but we need it urgently!".

The Regency styles, with peplums and pleats of our romanticism period were selling really well by this point. Melissa Caplan, Lee Sheldrick and Kim Bowen were my dressmakers, my stars of the future, soon to make names for themselves. We started producing ball gowns in taffeta, crinolines, petticoats and suits with pencil skirts and all kinds of shit in velvet including black altar boy suits. Along with my leather and suede, shawls and buccaneer waistcoats and long slashed jackets we had our new look. Stephen Jones was hanging around and one afternoon he stepped in to make his move and ask for a piece of the action so we put him in the basement downstairs. He made hats with feathers, berets and flamboyant styles that attracted plenty of attention and made him the star of the millinery word. The ostentatious and elaborate hats by Jones completed the PX look and he complemented us perfectly. On adding Steven Jones to PX2 and the Romantic Movement things could not have been going any better. There was one massive problem though, I was being an arse and was off my tits all day long. I'd become an addict and a casualty of the lifestyle I was living like many people in the creative world. I was another contender for biggest twat and it finally hit me back.

Paris nights with Steve Strange

By 81 Steve Strange was moving on. The glorious days of the Blitz Club were over and likewise, the glory of my reign over London's Covent Garden. My New Romantic clothes shop PX had lost its taste and appeal for me. I was changing at exactly the same moment that would announce the end of the New Romantics for both me and Steve, and now my focus was back on the King's Road, Chelsea to redesign the BOY shop and create the 80s dream. For Steve a new opportunity had arisen in London's Camden as he was about to launch the opening of The Camden Palace which quickly became the biggest hot spot for new music and style driven by Steve and his mate Rusty Egan. It would hit London during the dawn of the 80s with artists like Madonna, Grace Jones and Michael Jackson heading the bill at their Camden venue. I had been an influence on Steve in many ways including mentoring him in Paris. I had taken Steve on many trips to my favourite club Le Palace where he had fallen in love with Parisian nights and all the boys the two of us met there. He was inspired enough to rush back to London and begin creating London's own answer to those heady days we had spent on the streets of Paris. I went on to open the biggest new club scene in Paris when I opened the BOY club there, albeit unwittingly in partnership with the local mafia!

Leaving

Julia was spending more time with me in Endell Street and just before my leaving PX there was a last trip down to the South of France with my girlfriend Helen and Julia which may have just been the final nail in the coffin of the relationship, I became more attached to Julia and it didn't go unnoticed. I'd reached the point of the pleasure and the pain, I was falling more in love with Julia and she and I were getting totally out of control with our drinking. She had become my muse and confidante. She was yet another obsession as if I didn't have enough fucking obsessions already. Once I make up my mind about something it ends up being crash or burn, the agony and ecstasy, she'll know what I mean. So soon after that I was flung out of my home and business which has become a common occurrence in my life. So, with a cocktail of booze, drugs, obsessions, negative introspection and a touch of melancholy I was out on my ear. I realised I had to do something about it. If it had been these days I would have gone to rehab but there wasn't such a thing back then so I packed up my car and forced myself to endure my own personal rehab and could only hope that I would survive it. I had to stop or I would end up killing myself, so I felt the only thing was to get out of London.

I decided to move down to the south coast and headed to a small village just outside Brighton, I found a big old 1930's house right by the coast on the edge of a cliff with some grounds that I could wander around in. I had no choice but to go cold turkey. I was sick and shaking for months and life was absolute shit. It's bad when you get the DT's, you start hallucinating and freaking out. I discovered that the house was in an area that people went to commit suicide by throwing themselves over the cliff. It was definitely not a fucking positive experience.

I tried driving to London but each time I did I only got half way there and had to head back. I couldn't face it and knew that London wouldn't do me any good. I had to separate myself from all the addictions that were still there. I guess this hell went on for a few months, it was hard to tell how long I'd been holed up there. Finally, there was light at the end of the tunnel, I started to regain my sanity and strength. Eventually I gathered the balls to head back to London when out of nowhere I got a call from John Krivine asking if I'd like to work with him on taking BOY to the next level. I wasn't sure how it would go and initially I was worried that I'd not be up to the task but I wanted to go back and it felt right.

Life has no second act anyway. I'd been thrown out of my life with Helen, I was on my own and I was over PX and the whole Romantic scene, I knew I was ready to go back to the King's Road and my home at BOY. BOY needed me and I needed BOY. Princess Julia had stayed with the old gang so it was time to move on. People I had known before now hated me, I'd sure paid the price, I'd even begun doubting myself. As it turned out I was about to enjoy huge success and do some of my best work ever. Helen lost her grip on PX and it folded a year later but Julia always had star quality and still does.

The Batcave

In 1982 London went Gothic, it was yet another alternative subculture. Unlike now, they came thick and fast in those days. The difference between Punk and Goth was all about the attitude. Punk had always been quite violent with lots of spitting, pushing, pogoing and moshing. The Blitz club had been all about posing and who was or wasn't cool enough to be part of the scene, the crowd there took themselves very seriously. Goth was both extrovert and introvert, it was ok to just be yourself and enjoy the dark side but it was actually fun too. It was all about attitude and individualism. I imagine to outsiders it probably looked pretty strange but we were used to that. The Goths would go creeping around London's West End and make their way to the Batcave. The emaciated shapes of packs of Goths, like aliens, sex aliens, skulking through street trash. Deformed bodies with chains and cross jewellery in black clothing, PVC pants, black boots and hair shaved up the sides, non-binary looks, Loving the Alien.

All the early London Goths like the guys from Specimen who ran the club, Steve Severin, Marc Almond and Nick Cave would be seen there. Batcave music was really important, it was very selective and featured bands like Bauhaus, The Meteors, Sex Gang Children, The Virgin Prunes, Patti Paladin, Southern Death Cult and Alien Sex Fiend. There were super 8 films running on repeat and dark cabaret performances in the old theatre.

What a time to be alive, like the movie that never was, the movie that should have been ......too fast to live too young to die. There were always endless rumours of who would be in the club that night. The Batcave was the place to spot the likes of New Order, Robert Smith, Siouxsie and the Banshees and Johnny Slut who became a Goth style icon. They would all be huddled amongst the spider netting, movie screens and blackness. Twisted contouring bodies hanging from the stairs, laying or moving together on the dance floor.

I took some of my favourite girls to the Batcave. Ankie and Polly are the two I remember the most. I met Ankie in an old-fashioned way because she wrote me a letter which she sent to me at BOY. I went to pick her up on the East Coast of England at the seaport where the boats come in from Amsterdam. She was Swedish or Norwegian, not sure which. She was a model and fabulous looking. When we first met I couldn't have missed her as she was like an alien! As we drove back into London the radio was playing Our House by Madness, the funny thing about songs like this is they so suited the time we were living in. It made the drive back seem even more important. It was so fucking London, it was so right.

I loved taking her to the Batcave. We had so much fun there and the music was really good. They tried playing the Sex Pistols once but it emptied the dance floor. I remember it so well, I knew more than ever that Punk was definitely dead. The Batcave was now where the alternative, underground scene was and the music was the sound of the dark side. It felt so perfect at two in the morning to be walking in the shadows of a dark, misty London dressed as Goths. We were the "humans" that invaded London town with all the finery of Gotham, something that all the later Goths would never experience.

My time spent in the Batcave was a mixture of innocence and extremism, two things which have been most important in the longevity of Goth culture. The main reason for its popularity is that it never became a commodity or commercialised. It's a real movement. Staunch Punks could not deal with it, it went completely over the heads of Westwood, McLaren and so many others. Goth really suited BOY as it wasn't lifted from the USA. It was beautifully English and had a transsexual quality to it which made it far more desirable to me in design terms. The upstart of the fashion world, Jean Paul Gaultier studied it as a serious movement.

The mythology that surrounds the Batcave is stuff of legend yet it really was all that and much, much more. Despite being associated with death, sex and fetishism, Goth itself was liberating and one of the most copied movements of all time. It incorporated the image of desire, of expression, of anti-establishment. It was an attitude to life and living and it was also simply about having fun and dressing up. I'm so pleased to have been part of it.

Back to BOY

So, John Krivine and I met up and the two of us hit it off again straight away. He was always such a great guy and he had been keeping BOY warm for me. We were off and running , partners in crime once more and I jumped straight back in. I needed a place to live and John was living at Dolphin Square and knew of a barge for sale on the river, right next door to Westminster. I loved the idea of living on a boat plus it was close to Chelsea, the West End and Soho so it was perfect.

It was a Thames sailing barge and there are only a few left in the world now, GREAT! The downside was it came with a catch. I could buy the boat to get the mooring rights on the river but the Thames Water Authority wanted it removed as it was so old and was literally sinking. It needed to be moved as it was also becoming a danger to other vessels. The problem was they wouldn't actually allow me to move it as it could potentially foul the Thames if it sunk. As it happens and by good fortune we met a mad pirate with a tugboat. He told me that for £500 he would cut the ropes with an axe and tow the old girl away in the middle of the night. I agreed and took the risk that he would get it out of London without it sinking. It was quite an eerie moment to see the huge tug boat with its fog lights glowing through the mist, towing away this big motherfucker of a Thames Barge off into the night.

Somehow no one noticed it had gone and I have no fucking idea what happened to it, it could have ended up anywhere, maybe it's at the bottom of the Estuary. There was now an empty mooring so I needed a new boat to fill it. John and I took a trip to Amsterdam. We found a big Dutch barge that I liked and I paid a captain to bring it over to London. Again, we didn't know if the delivery would happen, we'd paid the guy the money and now we had to wait, holding our breath in anticipation of the new vessel turning up. It arrived one day moving steadily up the river, the captain pulled it up alongside the mooring at Dolphin Square and tied the ropes to the bank of the Thames. I had a new home in one of best locations in London, right opposite the stuffy old MP's

at Westminster. I was back at BOY with my old mate JK, I'd sorted myself out and got over my addictions and I was clean and sober which was new territory for me. This was going to be interesting.

Some say that they've travelled all over the world, and that it's overrated. My shop was all I ever needed because the world came to me. I never needed to travel much back then as amazingly everyone DID want to come to me! One morning at BOY, I found two Scottish girls sitting half asleep in the doorway. I opened up the shop, not talking to them very much, it was just understood that kids hanging around outside was a part of my day. By that evening the two girls were on board my new Dutch barge, they immediately became my crew and the barge became party central. They would climb the gates to get to the boat in the dead of night, boys and girls hanging around, 24 hours a day. I belonged to a privileged world that until then I had thought was only for The Rolling Stones or Led Zeppelin. I didn't really analyse this until I started writing this book. I would often sit on deck or in the wheelhouse, just watching London at all hours, Kiss FM blasting tunes like "Last Night a DJ Saved My Life". I was definitely living the dream. While the boat was gently bobbing up and down, side to side on the Thames, it was hard for me to get a grip on reality.

I had also just taken delivery of my brand new white-on-white Golf Turbo Cabriolet that some girl said looked like a fridge! It was THE car back then, as it happens Princess Diana had bought the same car on the same day, I'm not sure if that's cool or ironic. I was actually lucky to have the thing because when the salesman delivered it, he was informed by my accountant that a further discount was expected despite having already agreed terms, it made the salesman so angry that he threw the keys into the Thames. Anyway, it was now parked outside on the driveway next to the boat. Alongside the mooring there were tennis courts, for which I had the keys. There was also a swimming pool and the Archbishop of Westminster would swim there every morning, what a riot! This was Dolphin Square, one of the most prestigious areas of London, I was being watched by the pervy politicians though who secretly loved to spy on me with all the queer boys and girls dressed in latex that would clamber onto the boat every night. I remember thinking "Fuck off, this can't all be mine!".

It wasn't long before complaints were made about me and the debauched behaviour that had been reported by the pervy old Westminster boys (they were just pissed off that I was having all the fun). I was pulled up in front of the Dolphin Square committee who said I had to go, so my party barge went up for sale. Adam Faith came to view it but was worried about his kids falling overboard, in the end it was sold to some famous writer. It was time to leave Dolphin Square and head to the heart of Chelsea.

The Knack

I'd felt like becoming a Chelsea Sloane Ranger anyway so I responded to an advert for a Chelsea home to rent. As I'd come from Leicester, the Borough of Chelsea seemed like somewhere I was never going to live. It's posh round there, full of Chelsea tractors and women with expensive clothes and £1,000 handbags whose husbands are shagging the nanny. The idea of living in Chelsea with that lot was something that ordinarily I'd hate but it was the fact that someone like me shouldn't be living there that made me wanna live there all the more. I knew I had to look the part, so it was off with bondage trousers and on with the Michael Caine glasses and Burberry Mac. Maybe the white-on-white convertible BMW helped. Whatever the reason I got the gig and the white Chelsea mews house was all mine!

I knew it probably wouldn't last too long so I was just grabbing everything I could while it was on offer and who could blame me? One day I pulled up in the mews with the gang, top down on the convertible. We looked like extras out of a movie like Richard Lester's "The Knack and How to Get It' or Blow Up, staring David Hemmings or maybe even Frankie Goes to Hollywood's video for RELAX. Gone was the city boy look, instead we all piled out of the car dressed in bondage, black polished latex rubber and thigh high boots, this was essential day wear on the King's Road and we couldn't let our public down, they expected us to dress that way any hour of the day or night (Note...RELAX was a hit some years later but we were the template for the future) I'm not sure if the staunchly conservative locals in the neighbourhood saw it that way.

Having left the car parked halfway up the pavement with the top down all night we caused a great deal of curtain twitching the following morning when the young 'Punkettes' jumped in the car with a clatter of stilettos, clinking of chains and a flurry of big hair in various crazy colours, and we set off towards BOY, which was about four minutes away – screaming out of the mews side street and onto the King's Road whilst white van man hollered comments like "Wanker".

Here I was living moments from the shop…yeah, easy living in Chelsea, who the fuck would have thought it? As BOY went from strength to strength, I was going wild. I couldn't get enough, I knew I'd made it, I was a star, a Jack the Lad, a T-Rex, a Michael Caine.

No regrets
(Rants, Raves and Revolutions)

I'm a visual person, I need visual stimulation. I also need clever technology. I was first on the block to get a Commodore Console, and I made sure that I bought all the best games; I had Packman, Space Invaders, Donkey Kong…….but I immediately got into staying up for 36-hour stints, playing games non-stop. I'm also an obsessive and an addict, it was always about the danger, we were the first gamers on the block, and we were hooked. I'd have the TV on or maybe even two TV's as well as the console, and I'd be recording stuff on the VCR at the same time. It was mad. People dropped in and couldn't believe we were still up, with no sleep.

I'd had other addictions, the worst being Bucks Fizz (champagne and orange juice). I figured it was safe and kind of healthy, because of the orange juice, but I was drinking four bottles a night. Every night Steve Strange and I would hit all the nightclubs, mainly because he was obsessed with dressing up and showing off, but so he should have been. During this time Steve was my model and ran my PX London store, so every club loved it when we just turned up, being waved in ahead of the queue by the doormen and immediately being given a bottle of champers.

One of the worst clubs for this was up West on a Sunday night, it was £8 to get in and free champagne all night. The Embassy, that was THE place. Sunday nights were coolest, if you were there it meant you were someone or you were going to be someone, fame could happen overnight back then. It's where we stumbled upon Marilyn, as he came running up to us, screaming about how amazing we looked.

Another place was Legends, that was also a great club. Princess Julia was in our gang at that time and she came everywhere with us. She fancied a girl I was with, who was completely over the top (I only liked to hang out with amazing people, not necessarily pretty, just unique) and I loved being with Julia so I took them both everywhere. She was someone who along with Steve, was destined for stardom and she was great to have around. I was hooked in by her. We used to get really mashed together, to the point where it got totally insane – sometimes she would throw shoes at my window, shouting in her best cockney "Steph, Steph, let's go out".

I met her at Legends once, years later, during the acid rave period and she was the DJ! I was with some people, Julia and I were a bit nervous of each other but I guess we were both moving on, and what was done was done. I could never forget her, but my life was crazy. I was throwing parties in Paris, Ibiza, St. Tropez and everywhere else. There was a young French boy hanging around me by then, and a girl called Lisa, who was a transsexual and all over us. Things were moving up for me. Like that movie about Studio 54, only it was like being in my own movie. I just couldn't stop doing everything. I couldn't resist amazing situations. I would just dive in, head first. I was living in Chelsea, so why not?

The Boy Organisation

It was the 80's, and suddenly there was a thing called the media; there were two new TV channels so now we had four channels AND breakfast TV. We entered a new world of the 'celebrity'. We had left the dark ages of the 70's behind and things really were beginning to go POP! This was the perfect time for me to come out from the underworld, the underground of alternative dress and music, of Punks and Goths. I wanted to become over ground, artists like Madonna were starting to appear on the scene with her Goth meets baby doll styling. This was a perfect time for BOY. It was as if the script had been written for me, and from this point on the streets were literally paved with gold.

I hadn't even realised that there had been a recession going on in the U.K, we didn't care about politics. It was all bollocks, this stuff about Punks being political; the Sex Pistols were just Malcolm's new Bay City Rollers! Even The Clash said they knew nothing about politics or even who the Prime Minister was. None of us did. We were the new political party of success and fuck the government, whoever they were. Funny thing was, Margaret Thatcher, as much as we hated her, actually fitted right into our new world and even lived in Flood Street just up the road from BOY. She became a kind of celebrity herself.

It was like a fairy tale. I arrived back at the perfect moment; it felt as though BOY had been waiting for me. John had asked me to come back because he was still selling the Punk look, and although there was still a big Punk following, he knew I could change it up and change it up I did. Just like in '76 when I pissed off all the Acme soul boys by going Punk, here I was again, this time pissing off the Punks and the New Romantics but I did it in a clever way by evolving into Goth first.

Goth was good; it had a mutated Punk attitude, but with a new flair, it will always be present in everything we do and the way we live our lives. It sometimes gets overlooked by many, actually by almost everyone. I mean we all wear black now and for some people their entire world is black and as a creative designer of life I know this. Goth, like the Batcave and Dark Wave is not at all depressing. It's liberating and one of the most copied movements of all time. It's an image of desire, of expression, of anti-establishment. It was an attitude to life and the living and it was about having fun dressing up.

Goth felt like the right way to bring me back into things, it felt like a long way from the Blitz Club and the Punk scene. It was 1982 and all that stuff was over, to me it was well and truly dead, it hadn't occurred to everyone else by then but they soon realised that I'd gone. The Goth scene also mixed things up with the northern music sound that was hitting the south at the same time. This crossover would carry on for years after, going right up to the late 80's and 90's with bands like Soft Cell, The Fall, The Smiths and New Order. It was another very British scene and I loved it and it fell right into my hands, like a Flock of Seagulls meets Yazoo.

I knew that I had drifted away from Punk completely, and from Vivienne and Malcolm, they never seemed to know what was going on out on the street anyway, they were too art school; not street at all. They had one last bash at creating a cult, which I had actually already done back at PX in 1979 with the birth of New Romantics, Steve Strange and the Blitz Kids. Viv and Malc called their collection Pirates, but that was 3 years after I created my Buccaneer look much favoured by the Spandau boys and my mate Steve. Actually, I was totally bored of all that by then. Malcolm was a genius at creating publicity though and once again gave us a taste of his 'media circus' by creating bands like Adam and the Ants and Bow Wow Wow, although he totally pillaged the ideas from me. That scene was all Malcolm, he was doing his Larry Parnes the impresario bit, typically though it was accredited to them both, same ole story.

I was a bit nervous about what was to come next and how it would work out going back to my old haunt. There were a few people driving the scene in London at the time, they moved from being

Acme Soul Boys to Punks then from Punks to New Romantics. They were the ones that knew what the next thing was and it changed fucking fast back then. The New Romantic movement was almost over, and the romantic bands were looking dated, but the ones that knew, that really knew, followed me back to BOY especially Boy George and later Steve Strange, and there were plenty of others that were keeping an eye on what I was up to.

JK took me over to the new HQ which was once again in South London. It had some advantages as it was huge and it was where we did much of the Goth shoot (Black catalogue 1982). It was very close to the river by Vauxhall, so the opposite side of London to Covent Garden where I'd been hiding out for a few years. There was plenty of action around there, it was starting to become an edgy area not too far from Brixton, and a gay community was springing up. There was the Vauxhall Tavern which was full of queer cowboy clones with hankies in their back pockets, moustaches and checked shirts. Later the whole area would rocket up in value but no one would have guessed it at the time of the early 80's. It became party central for gay clubs and fetish joints and I loved it.

I bought a minivan and started delivering cloth to our machinist then we set up a printing table, then a northern girl just turned up out of nowhere and started designing. Once I drove home with her back up North, I think it was Leeds but it could have been Manchester. I didn't go North that much anymore but it still had a certain charm and a vibrant music scene with loads of bands. Her place was great, it had a couple of rooms that she shared with another girl and was typical of a northern house on a typical northern street. I think it was raining and there were dirty panties everywhere with Smiths posters on the walls, the whole place was fab.

Soon after this BOY HQ moved again when we took a place on the King's Road almost opposite the BOY shop. We set everything up properly this time with several sewing machines and printing tables. This was where I designed the BOY Eagle and BOY LONDON artwork with the help of Mark who was running the printing side of things. We were now functioning as close to a fashion organization as we could and we kicked it!

Back then getting hold of a work and studio space was relatively easy even considering it was Chelsea. You'd need to be a fucking multi-millionaire to get a shoe box there nowadays. It was a great time to be back in London though as people like Boy George and John Moss would drop in on us just because they wanted to hang out. I remember taking a call from a boy who said he could do so much more than we were with our designs and actually told me our clothes were shit. I liked his fucking nerve and the sound of his voice so I invited him over. I offered him a job on the spot, turned out he was a rampant gay boy and within minutes of starting to work for us he was having sex in the staff toilet!

So now we really were up and running, although none of us had any idea what we were doing but it worked. To be honest I'm not sure the rest of the fashion world knew what they were doing at the time either. It was all very DIY for us back then and we didn't follow the established idea of clothing design, so I suppose we were ahead of the game in a way. Suddenly there was a real interest in what was happening at BOY and we were bombarded with business proposals from Australia to Japan. It was weird as most of the interested parties that approached us had no idea about who or what we were or how we were doing it as it was all so new, but all I cared about was that we had become busy and we were bringing the cash in.

BOY was now a proper business. We were getting the Goth scene going which, much like back in the days of Punk, we were making up everything as we were going along, despite this the high street shops and multiples just couldn't keep up with us.

Around this time BOY began attracting copycat shops and units like Beaufort Market that opened down the bottom of the King's Road. It was situated right between Vivienne and Malcolm's shop and BOY. Anyway, it was set up as a Punk, new wave, alternative market in a large building and it became very busy. Initially I wasn't too happy about it as it felt like they were trying to muscle in on our game and copy our formula. In the end I didn't care as it didn't hurt our business and in fact it helped to make the King's Road THE alternative area of London and solidified it as the only place to be. Beaufort Market would finally close down, with Punks demonstrating, police outside waiting for trouble and The Clash playing. The Clash were always playing somewhere.... Anyway, now it's all just dust, a distant memory.

By now the King's Road was the playground of the fashionable, the self-styled and flamboyant dressers from the alternative scenes and BOY was the epicentre of all of this. During the week the street was overrun with Chelsea girls, bands, pop stars, fashion stylists and at the weekends it was crazy with swarms of dressed up kids, crowding the pavements, walking down the centre of the road, parading up and down and congregating around BOY, oblivious to everyone around them apart from the other like-minded tribes. The public just stood and stared at this migration of the weekend flock that had descended on Chelsea like pink Flamingos showing off their finery. British style ruled the world again, I was back at the wheel and I had a feeling this version of BOY was going to be something really big, in fact it probably ended up being my biggest achievement, certainly the most memorable at the very least.

So, I was fully established once again in Chelsea and ready for whatever life threw at me. I was literally ready for anything, in fact I was really looking forward to it. I'd just had the ride of my life between 73 and 83, I'd created three legendary moments in pop history from Acme Attractions, with its British Soul Boys, to the Punk underground and alternative New Wave of early BOY and onwards and upwards to PX and the New Romantic scene. It was non-stop, sometimes unbelievable, other times extraordinary but it never stopped, not for one minute. I hadn't even had a chance to let it sink in. It was just like a conveyor belt of fashion, cars, girls, sex, clubbing. I'd just had the romance of living on a boat on the Thames and going out with Goth girls.

I'd lived all over London and now I was on my own again and ready for more. I'd come back full circle and I was living in Chelsea just across the road from the BOY shop. I had a big challenge ahead of me as I knew I needed to be on top of my game and transform BOY into something really special, I was 'tense and nervous" but that's a good energy, and I was ready to get the party started.

So, start I did, with some quick creative moves I changed BOY'S imagery turning it around to achieve maximum impact which really spiked interest in the brand. I wanted the interior to have an edgy, post-Punk feel, it was what set BOY apart from the rest and made us unique. I sprayed up mannequins in gloss red, dressed them in latex rubber and black PVC and hung heavy chrome chains from the ceiling using the theatre as my inspiration. We started hand-printing rolls of cloth and T-shirts, dying army shirts black then adding on straps, clips and rings. I was bringing the feel of the Batcave to the shop with the help of Gail, a young designer who I was working with at the time. I'd designed a selection of hand printed fabrics, some tribal, some with bats, spiders, crucifixes, skulls and of course there were the essential black dresses, black tops and black trousers. My first look was complete and once again BOY had the strongest image in town.

We were wicked and the rest of the world could only watch and wonder what this upstart cunt was gonna think of next. Job done!

They were the Smash Hits years. Smash Hits was the paper magazine that informed kids about what was going on in music, with fan worship, bands and pop stars. Sounds shit now but it wasn't, it was fresh, nobody had published anything like it before. There was a whole plethora of publications, from Mark's Sniffin Glue fanzines, to the New Music Express, Melody Maker and right up to Smash Hits. They were informative and culturally relevant. It felt kinda personal as there wasn't much else out there and along with the launch of MTV we lived in our own unique world that was breaking down barriers and kicking down doors at a breakneck speed. We felt in control, nothing could touch us, we were the Kings and Queens of it all and when the Saturday crowds started coming to BOY in their hundreds BOY itself became like a pop star and I became the Svengali, the front man, the puppet master. I was at the heart of the controls and it felt fucking immense, right up there on top of the world!

BOY BIOGRAPHY

STARTED IN 77/76 KINGS ROAD

Is known as the shop that created "Punk". Amongst the 'blue & green' hair it swept the pop industry from Great Britain to Japan. Billy Idol worked in the shop - Sid Vicious and Johnny Rotton would hang out there. The list of stars is endless, Bob Geldof, The Stones etc. etc.

Within a couple of successful image years, BOY became a cult name across much of the world.

It became a tourist haven for all the young people and the legend went on. BOY became internationaly known when BOY was listed in the tourist guides next to Buckingham Palace. BOY had now become famous.

The year that followed crowds caused chaos on the street. They became so big that doormen were employed to hold the crowds back.

By the 80's BOY had to change its format and update its image.

that even more pop/fashion people became involved.
The Pet Shop Boys began the next phase and quickly most
Pop stars became involved

Then Boy George!

All this time Boy opened another store, the shops became
even busier (see Boy steel shot). Most countries by
now were aware of its appeal. This phase 2 went
on for 5 years. Again the look needed turning
around, this time to an even younger audience + sportswear
+ new pop heroes.

It worked again, The magazines flocked in and
the first of the new breed of stars chose to wear Boy
ie. YAZ, S. Express.

The major Global promotion for Boy was the catalogue
together with the history/press/+ fashion shows.
From the catalogues the enquiries came from every
corner of the Globe, But with this came unforseen
problems. Quickly fortune seekers attatched themselves to us,
the rest you know. It was impossible to control and
a cry for help went out. This is the story so far.!

Boy Catalogues

My next priority was to shoot the BOY catalogue. I called it the Big Black Catalogue and I used characters like Jonny Slut the iconic Goth as my model. I had it printed in black and white to reflect my mood. As I said, some of it was shot at the old South London HQ. The rest in central London around Leicester Square and Eros at Piccadilly Circus. Then out and about in the back streets, high streets, bus stops, grave yards and trash cans of London. It really reflected the vibe of what "our" city felt like back then. It's now a very sought- after collector's piece and considered one of the turning points in the history of BOY.

The Big Black Catalogue was the first of our mail order catalogues for the 80's, there must have been 20 altogether. Boy George modelled for us a few times, as well as Mandy Smith, soon to infamous for her dalliance with Bill Wyman of The Stones and the delightful Stacey Smith who later married the 80's star Paul Young. There were boys and girls from the streets and gay Skinheads. The clothing was so different from anything else around at the time and we used badges

and logos in a unique way, which was part of the reason for BOY's ongoing fame. I enlisted the very talented conceptual stylist Judy Blame to style many of the shoots and he added his couture safety pins to complete the look. No other fashion company had the foresight to do anything like this. We were pushing the boundaries, using androgynous models who were not just a symbol of youth but were also changing attitudes. I was very involved in creating these catalogues and was always excited about how far we could push our concepts. Our fans were blown away by the images. BOY has been called THE gay label, we were definitely at the forefront of the gay movement. I didn't really think about that, it never even occurred to me, all I knew was I was always right even when I was wrong! I had this desire for the world to see my work and these catalogues were the perfect tool. Now regarded as art and art photography, each image has become iconic, a visually accurate account of how things looked back then. They not only represent the BOY culture but also a history of style from some of fashions most influential decades.

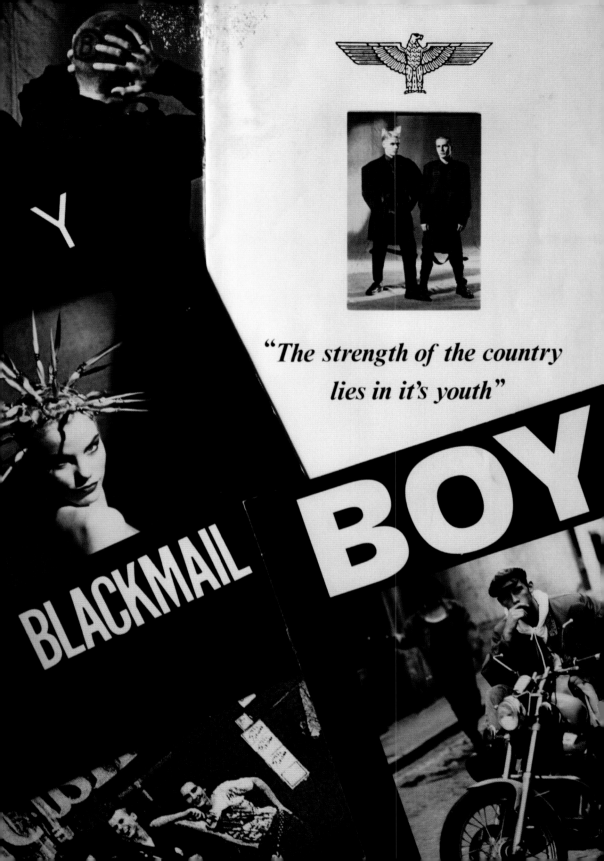

Y

"The strength of the country lies in it's youth"

BLACKMAIL BOY

iNtiMACy

ExhiBitiOniSm

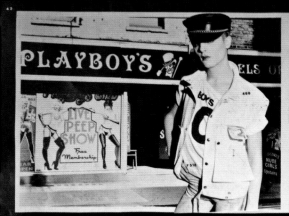

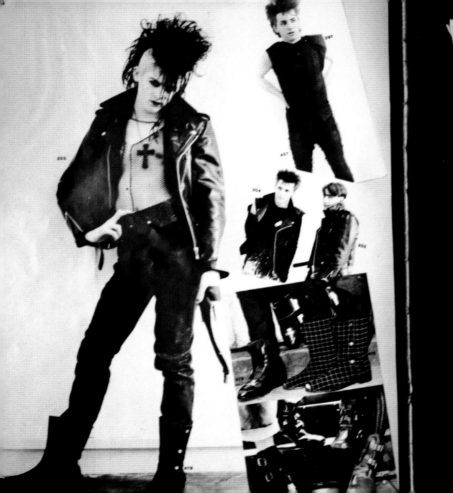

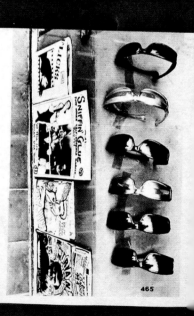

Boy London

The next thing I wanted to do was concentrate on making the BOY logo stronger. I mean BOY was more than a good enough name but it had been up outside the shop for ten years by now and I felt I needed to tweak it a bit, give it something extra, I just didn't know what. The logo needed to shout about who we were and what we represented. I didn't know anything about 'aggressive' marketing but everybody THOUGHT I did and they were looking, waiting and watching me. I had to get my shit together and do something about it, to prove to the world that I was the 'chosen one' but fuck me, at times it sure was tough.

Paul McCartney once said the moment you know when you've got a hit record is when the window cleaner is whistling your tune. I had a mountain to climb but just like I had in the past, I knew it would come together this time too. My print boys were fucking around on the print table one day when they called me in and asked what were the ideals BOY originally stood for, like our motto 'The Strength of the Country is in its Youth'. We took this eagle that we'd all been looking at in the history books and we dropped BOY underneath it, I said, "can we get its claws like sitting on it?". The guys set to it and when I saw the finished design, I said "fuck me, we got it!". It sent shivers down my neck and as I've said again and again, the rest is history. So, I told them to print some T-shirts up as quickly as possible as I couldn't wait to see the finished pieces. We called our method of working vertical, meaning we would work on an idea in the morning and literally have the designs on the rails and for sale by the afternoon, this is the way I've tried to work ever since, it has its drawbacks but its fucking exciting.

Now around the same time, maybe slightly later, interested parties started 'knocking at my door and ringing my bell' (Mr McCartney again). They wanted to know if they could buy wholesale from us for their stores around the world. The Americans were always there pretty damn fast and they had this horrible turn of phrase and kept calling me up saying stuff like 'hey, can we get some of these shirts from BOY of London'! I immediately thought ok, I can do a play on words here and do a shirt print called BOY LONDON in fact I'll get them printed right now. At least I think I heard myself saying it, or was it the voice of the devil inside me? Either way, print them we did and the second biggest BOY design was born. Amen.

Boys keep swinging

As I was contemplating where and how my new designs for the BOY Eagle should first be presented to the world I came up with a capsule collection with small eagles strategically placed all over the garments. They were kinda Laura Ashley meets the Third Reich, or maybe a Roman soldier if we're going to play it safe, although there was nothing safe about Roman soldiers either, especially if you were a Christian.

I'd made a quick collection in black with a gold print which included mini-skirts, leggings, vests and crop tops. A mate of mine called Dave was living in Birmingham at the time and said, "why don't cha cum up and we'll put on a fashion show, cos I know everyone up here and everyone knows me'. He had an event planned with some designers and a band from Birmingham called Fashion. So up I went with the new collections and met the models, all the girls were really enthusiastic and excited. The night was going well and everyone was waiting for the BOY show, as Bowie's Boys Keep Swinging started to blast out, my models came alive and the world's first viewing of the Eagle collection happened on a back street in Birmingham almost completely unannounced and you can guess how much I liked that, it was so radical and Punk!

The boy is back in town

At that moment in time I was fearless and I seemed to have a gift. Of course, I could fall and stumble at any moment but I was still young enough to not think about that too much. I was gathering a team of good sample machinists around me, so now we could design stuff and produce the garments in-house. There seemed to be a steady flow of kids coming into BOY who were inexperienced but willing to learn so I gave them the chance to work with me while I directed everything. We were making great headway and things were progressing quickly on the King's Road. It was the perfect move to have our work studio directly opposite the shop so people would pop in and out all day. We would work on new ideas for prints, mainly for T-shirts, as that was our strength. Whether it was Bowie or Siouxsie or a statement T, they were selling like fucking hot cakes. We were really getting a great look together.

BOY was becoming an essential part of the new crowd, I found it weird that I had got 'the crowd' to follow me from the King's Road to Covent Garden then all the way back to the King's Road. That's exactly what happened though and two of the biggest names to follow me were Boy George and the Pet Shop Boys. It was freaky. I suppose Viv and Malcolm helped a bit but it took them some time to catch up and by then I was "the Emperor of all that surrounded me", the "chairman of the board' to quote a great song. I was feeling creative, I was back on board the ship called BOY!

On one particular Saturday at the height of Boy George mania, we were ready for another massively busy day. Saturday's always felt different somehow, we knew there would be hordes of 'Saturday shoppers' some regular, some on a day trip to the mecca of style, the King's Road, London SW3. What we didn't know when we opened for business on that particular Saturday, was that George and his friends Tranny Paul and our favourite queen Philip Sallon were making their way down the street with a film crew whilst being interviewed by US chatshow queen Barbara Walters. They trooped in, blinding lights following their every move, with George who was pulling various items of clothing from the rails, making his usual caustic comments. Seconds later, both the shop and the street were under siege, with the manic Saturday

traffic halted and crowds of screaming and cheering people trying to get a glimpse of the enigma that was Boy George. With the filming over and knowing that there was no way he was going to get out of the front door alive, I let George and his entourage out through the back door, slowly the crowds buggered off and we went back to a regular mental Saturday.

No two days at BOY were the same and it's only natural that some days were better than others. We always had to get set up for business, reorganising rails, dressing windows, reordering stock that was selling fast. A key item that we needed to stay on top of were the now iconic BOY bags. When I first designed them, they were white with the BOY LONDON logo in black. I switched them to clear bags so that the clothes were visible and along with the black and white BOY tags I created an entire package. I could never get enough of these bags. Customers who came from all over the world were obsessive about the label and would go as far as waiting for days on end or even cancelling flights back home if we couldn't give them their clothing in a fully loaded BOY bag!

Back to the story. So this was one of those Mondays where nothing much was likely to happen besides sorting shit out ready for another week and of course re ordering a ton of bags. I noticed something was happening outside so I looked up the street and saw a long, stretch limousine prowling slowly up The King's Road to the door of BOY, stopping right outside. The driver went around and opened the rear door. Who could this be? Was it royalty? Then we got our first glimpse of the limo's occupant. They were clearly determined to come right into BOY, I mean they were hardly going next door to Pepe fucking jeans! No, they were heading straight for the door and indeed they were royalty but a new kind of royalty. Someone whom even I thought was worth asking for an autograph from. Everyone in BOY was usually way too cool to ask for an autograph but this person was different. I had danced to her music as a young Mod in Leicester, her videos played constantly in BOY, this was the 80's she was at her peak, this was The Queen of fucking Motown, it was Diana Ross!

This was definitely a Manic Monday (RIP Prince).

Viv and Malc
(Rants, Raves and Revolutions)

BOY was the one shop that was in direct competition with SEX. We used to send Punk kids down the road to Viv and Malc when they asked us "Oi mate, got any of them T-shirts what the Pistols wear?" and on their return they'd say "Finks geezer, but what a load of tossers down that SEX shop. Like fuckin' schoolteachers or paedophiles or something".

Eventually, Vivienne and Malcolm's days came to an end. Vivienne of course would carry on, no longer influenced or advised by Malcolm so the great days of pop chaos were over for them. Vivienne ended up doing what she wanted to do – get away from those snotty, dishevelled, scruffy street urchins like Sid, and start making frocks!

So, their era was over and mine was just getting started. I often wonder what those two would have made of Ibiza. Nothing really, I guess, as they were so art school. They never got Mods, Goths and Soul Boys, and came very late to the party with their pirate look. So acid house would have gone right over their heads. I on the other hand was a kid from the street, but I had an Avant-Garde touch and BOY was always grittier.

In saying that, McLaren was the genius behind so much from that time but somehow a great deal of the truth has been lost to history and Westwood now gets the credit for much of it. I guess as Malcolm has been dead for some time now Viv will probably write him out completely in the end. Shame as he really was the ultimate trickster and Svengali. Both myself and McLaren used the King's Road as our manor, crib, territory, to parade our work, style, counter-culture and movements. McLaren was of course responsible for creating The Sex Pistols who immediately gained notoriety and infamy as THE best Punk band as well as one of the most influential bands in music history. Malcolm's influence on that era and beyond is immeasurable, he was the without a doubt the kind of character that doesn't come around too often.

The end of those two meant the coast was clear for me, it was unbelievable. I could see for miles and I was out there on my own, no competition, it was mad. There were shops like Jones, but they were selling labels from France and Italy. This was the heyday of French and Italian designer wear but in the UK, nobody could touch me.

There were some good shops down at World's End like Anthony Price, left over from the Roxy Music days. Although he was in a completely different market to me he had celebrity status and we loved it. His place was located somewhere between BOY and SEX. As I've always been really interested in retail and set design and stuff, to this day I still can't believe the interior Anthony created there. Punters would walk into a white cube which encompassed the shop but that was it, there was nothing else, just white walls and a white floor. That was already a pretty surreal sensation but then, out of nowhere, a hatch in the wall would open and out would come an arm holding a garment. Now I should check that this did actually happen as when I've told stories like this before I've been asked if I was still taking LSD and there are many stories like this coming up!

Andy Warhol looks a scream, hang him on my wall

Andy Warhol just appeared out of the blue on this one day and he just walked into my BOY shop unannounced. He had a little gang with him including Billy Boy and he came up to me and shook my hand, his handshake was very weak, I remember it well, and he was a little frail looking. He said the store was great and he proceeded to float around picking up various pieces and then to my surprise and delight he started trying things on. He walked around as if he was almost modelling the stuff then somebody said, "hey Andy, can we get some photos" and Andy said "yeah, sure, ok", so he posed for a few shots and paraded up and down the shop floor. We were getting some pretty good shots of him and he looked really good. I said, "hey Mr Andy Warhol what do you want me to do with these pictures?" And he replied "just use my face to make yourself some money" He also had some copies of his magazine Interview with him and asked me if I wanted one, of course I did! He signed two copies for me.

Those photos represent to me another piece of the never-ending story and history of BOY. Andy died unexpectedly a few years later, I was fucking privileged that I had the chance meet the great Andy Warhol, he was the absolute master of his time.

BOY
153 KING'S ROAD LONDON SW3
THE STRENGTH OF THE COUNTRY LIES IN
BOY

The BOY Club

The story of the BOY club is as strange as any of my BOY stories, for one thing it almost seems like it never happened. In 1976 I had met a French guy completely by chance at the market in Clignancourt. They called him the Indian, he was selling button badges from a small stall tucked away in the corner of the market. Clignancourt was one of my favourite places in Paris, it was huge and always really busy. It had different sections for the varied traders, some were pavement traders, others selling high end antiques. I would have lunch there in the chaotic restaurants with their sawdust floors. I felt like a bit player in a French film noir. It was a real portrait of Parisian life with every character imaginable walking, talking, eating, buying bric a brac and generally being Parisian.

So, I met the Indian, his stall was noticeable because it was so popular, it sold rock bands badges and associated merchandise and back in the 70's this was pretty unusual. We chatted and he was very animated, a bit of a character. I had just arrived in France and I knew nothing about Paris, he told me he was well connected and could help me sell my stock in all the best places around Paris. I had nothing to lose as these were the early days so I went along with the whole thing so as to get my foot in the door. Of course, dealings with the Indian got out of control real fast! It was cool being around him and he was kinda fun but he was a little hot headed. He had been banned from driving in the UK when he was caught over the limit after taking just about everything and on one occasion I was with him he took me to a travel agent he used in Paris, and the girl there wasn't too polite so he dived over the counter and started strangling her. When the police came we had to split pretty quickly.

I had said that he could do deals on my behalf with the BOY collection in Paris, but no matter what he could NOT open a fucking BOY club. Despite these instructions he took me one day to meet these two Corsican brothers who had a huge club in the city. They looked exactly like you would imagine; kind of swarthy, wearing leather coats and flashy watches, they looked more like Argentinian gun runners. The Indian argued that this would be the deal of a life time, it turned out they were associates of his and apparently, they had "acquired" the club, whatever that meant, and in Paris you just never knew. I felt sick inside, I just thought, what the fuck had he got me into. The meeting seemed to be going well, the club was a serious venue, it was a fairly prominent place with the capacity to fit about 2,000 punters. It was evening and the club was already open only the huge dancefloor was almost completely empty. The Corsican brothers asked me what I thought they could do to fix things, to make it cool. I replied that they should get some atmosphere going, maybe some dry ice and lights and stuff. Call it BOY, kill the fucking DJ, stop him playing Hawkwind, or whatever shit he was playing, throw some fashion parties BOY style, do some late gay nights and put some relevant DJ's in the house. A few weeks later the Indian told me they were ready to sign a deal which would include a free retail space so we struck a deal. So, the BOY club deal went ahead and as I said there was no way back, anyway the Indian had got me into this mess and sink or swim I was in it up to my neck so I figured here goes nothing.

The club became a massive success, most nights we had three changes of vibe, first up the regular clubbers, then the late night fashionable crowd and finally what they call the people of the night, the gay crowd and the trannies. The cash was rolling in and within a few months the BOY club became the top

club in Paris, even Elton John threw a party there. Over 1,000 people turned up every night, there was permanently a queue around the block and no one seemed to care that they were charging 100ff a drink! The club just kept going from strength to strength.

But as usual, there was a big downside to this arrangement, as I would experience time after time throughout my so-called career. My biggest fears had come true, it seemed that the Corsicans had put the word out that they would shoot me on sight if I turned up at the club or caused them any trouble, and what made it worse was that everyone I knew in Paris was going there but I definitely thought it was better to stay the fuck away from the place! Last I heard the Corsican brothers had got a bit cocky after gaining enormous credibility as a result of the success of the BOY CLUB and they'd headed off to Miami to muscle in on the club scene over there. More of that later.......

Down & out in Paris

I had unwittingly joined forces with the French Mafia. It was what I can only describe as a typically French situation but you have to understand what that means. By this point there was the BOY nightclub in Paris as well as boutiques in Les Halle's, Rue St Dennis, Paris and at the port at St Tropez. To understand everything about the French and their lifestyle would take a lifetime and I believe I've encountered just about every possible situation so much so that even most of the French don't know what I'm talking about.

The agreement to have a boutique in one of the best streets in Paris was set up between me and a guy called Mark who walked around smoking Gitanes cigarettes, he was very French. He told me 'we bring the walls (the shop) and you bring the fashion, and if your fashion sells we pay you and if not goodbye'. What he didn't tell me was he was owned and controlled by Jacques who was obviously mafia and also owned all the sex clubs in the area and probably everything else too. Anyway, Mark was OK and he was interested in my girls more than me so we set up shop, styled the windows, dressed the mannequins, brought in the stock and acquired a cash till. The French always had some old dragon lady working on the till, often their mother but occasionally a younger girl that dressed like a tart but that the French described as fashionable. She would be kitted out in high heel boots and regulation tight, bum clinging jeans.

Anyway, we were set, or should I say as well-set as could be expected. They wheeled in someone else's stock at the last minute that was really disgusting, probably for a mafia friend or someone whom they owed a favour to or who more likely owed them money, and so we opened. I didn't care so much about how it all went because I was used to the Punk world, which was completely different to the fashion business, in fact the French had absolutely no idea what was going on at all. Their idea of Punk was to wear a Saint Laurent suit jacket with the collar turned up and loosen their tie. Les femmes just wanted to look sexy so I was up against it from day one but I'd achieved my goal, my dream, I was a Parisian and for me that was the bollox. The Parisians might not have known anything much about Punk but they knew a lot of other shit, the regular stuff that brought tourists to Paris, the songs, the movies, (An American in Paris) one of the best and April in Paris is one of my favourite songs, Gene Kelly's dance moves were out there!

I never go to the shit stuff that tourist go to see, they're all assholes and destroy everything creative, I wanna kill them all……. Anyway, I never went up The Eiffel Tower although I drove past it a thousand times. My life involved hanging out at sidewalk cafes, ordering Coquille St. Jacques or oysters whilst reading some French fashion magazines, looking cool. One time recently I took two of my favourite girls to Paris.

They were young and up for anything. We drove through the night into Paris by dawn just how I like to do things. Miles Davis was purring out of the car radio. One great thing about the French is their obsession with jazz, as McLaren put it so succinctly "Jazz is Paris and Paris is Jazz". Whenever you turn on the radio in Paris you hear Dylan one minute, Sebastian Bach the next followed by Dizzy Gillespie. That's the Paris I love and back then I would just cruise around in my car by night. One time I was with a young, crazy Russian girl who I would fall head over heels in love with. We drove by the Seine on a misty autumn night with classical opera banging out of my speakers, we passed by eerie statues and monuments that were just possible to make out through the fog. She was screaming out opera and banging her hands on the dashboard. One time we were walking together on a French beach on a blowy, damp winters day and I told her that they had filmed 'A Man and a Woman' on this very beach. She asked me who the film director was but I couldn't remember, even though it's a favourite film of mine, especially the opening song which is so 60s and so French. Anyway, she flipped open her phone and called her parents in Moscow insisting they would know and sure enough they both came on the phone giving the answer, Claude Lelouch.

By avoiding tourists, I was in my Paris, I owned it. Eventually I realised that I needed a French lawyer for contracts and advice, especially when as time went on I was aware that my French partner Mark was no longer very prompt with his payments from the Paris BOY shop. After several months of insisting he had to pay up and getting nowhere I decided that my lawyers should press for payment. Finally, Mark sent a cheque for 200,000 FF, to clear the debt and it was deposited into my bank account, but it bounced, of course it fucking bounced! My lawyer explained to me that in France if you write out a cheque that is not honoured it's a criminal offence, so the next day she explained this to Mark who said he was sorry and would bring the cash over straight away. Now I don't know if any of you know or love Jacque Tati movies but this was a perfect example of French farce. My lawyer took a call late one afternoon as we were both sitting in her office waiting for the cash to arrive. We were informed that Mark was on his mobilette bike, one of those wonderful little black bikes with a tiny engine on the front that only the French could design, he was threading his way in, out and through the Parisian traffic with the cash stashed in his back pack. Anyway, sometime that afternoon the phone rang again only this time it was to inform us that unfortunately as Mark had been wending his way over to our office, an auto bus had knocked him off the bike and killed him ...hmmm very mafia and very French.

The BOY Cap

Everywhere I went in Paris, people would stare, I would go into designer boutiques and girls would know me, they would tell me what was selling and what wasn't. They were interested in what I was wearing as street fashion was slower to take off in Paris. I would wear British Knights, Travel Fox, and BOY hoodies from my store in London. I actually made my own fake Gucci and Chanel streetwear, I wanted to wear those brands but they didn't make streetwear so I thought, OK I'll just make the pieces myself. I would wear leather jeans that I was making in Leicester, it was hard to get hold of leather jeans in Paris. My look was different, they hadn't seen anyone that dressed like me before. I loved some French labels too, I was always into Gaultier and Gaultier

Junior, he had some really sweet numbers, real designer classics. The other thing I noticed was that nobody was selling cool caps, sure they had a million sporting the NY Dodgers and shit but I must have been the first person ever to make designer caps with a great logo. I came back to the UK with the idea that I would start producing BOY caps. Nobody really wore caps back then, so I started looking everywhere for a place that could make them. I'd nearly given up when I found this little factory in the North of England, they didn't trust me at first, like many others before them, but I persuaded them to try making me some samples and the rest, once again, is history. That little factory got rich and the Pet Shop Boys never looked back!

Les Bains Douches

I was now part of Paris, I was throwing parties, going to parties, doing fashion shows. I was living in a swanky apartment but was often cruising the streets day and night checking into beautiful hotels with girls and boys. I'd made it, I was living yet another dream.

I'd opened my own fashion boutique and even met the French mafia, I was made up. I threw an opening party at Les Bains Douches, Paris's coolest club. Their door policy was "Rich or poor, young or old, famous or unknown, but no ordinary people". This party was a first for me as it was being hosted by a big fashion magazine, it was like no experience I had ever had before although there have been many more parties like it since. In a very Parisian way as mentioned before, guests could not be ordinary. Everyone looked like a model or someone out of a French movie. Also, guests had to dine together at the long banqueting table. The party started out well. The cream of French Avant Garde society were there plus me and whoever the crew was that I'd taken with me. So, we're all scoffing away together in the style of Marie Antoinette's

"let them eat cake" and some of the girls had been getting pissed on the ole vintage champers and were now climbing onto the dining table and smashing glasses and china and lifting up their skirts and doing some dirty dancing. Since then I've noticed that kinda thing happens all the time at certain kinds of events, it's yet another 'French' thing. So, they quickly ended the dinner and led us downstairs into la discotheque. Oh, by the way there was a great piece of art at the dinner table, it was a big red neon lightning bolt that came from the ceiling, went through the dining table, then through the floor and on into the club downstairs. So, having been escorted downstairs we were left to party! It was as surreal as hell down there, there were dancers moving around on the floor but there was no music, I thought hello, what the fuck is going on, whatever it was it looked super cool, then I realised how to join in. You simply pulled down headphones that were suspended from the ceiling and put them on so you could hear the music, like an early silent disco.

Another thing about Paris is its very adult understanding of the surreal and of sexual fetishism. Later that night I saw people leaning at strange angles against a wall, some almost upside down and upon further investigation I found small holes had been drilled into the club walls in random areas, some up high where you'd need to stand on tiptoes to see through them and others lower down near the floor which you needed to lay down to access. It was an interesting study of human behaviour but what could be causing such a commotion? Sex of course, for behind the wall sex extremism was taking place. I thought it was so unique that much later I replicated the idea in a London fetish club that I designed called Torture Garden. In the end I was actually banned from the very same fucked up fetish club! To complete the tale of my debauched party night at Les Bains Douches, the most famous club in Paris, there was one last surreal treat and that was the pool. It was filled with the blackest water and whether intentionally or not there were pieces of smashed glass on the bottom so people were coming out of the water cut and bleeding. The whole place was fucking great, it was like anarchy, meets art, meets voyeurism!

The slap

What I'd been doing was playing Paris and Italy at their own game. I could see I was never gonna beat them as they had superior manufacturing skills, better quality cloth and great fabric design, but just like in the music business the UK had an edge. For us it was all about teenagers and I could design T-shirts and streetwear that left the French standing still as this was a market I knew extremely well and the French and Italians knew nothing about at all. We were starting to do fashion trade shows in Paris and I ended up having a love hate relationship with Paris at show time. I mean I loved the idea of having to go to Paris, and at any other time you couldn't drag me away as any excuse to go there was excuse enough.

Unfortunately, I found the overwhelming commercialism of it all was really disappointing. There were so many assholes around it really wasn't my scene. I remember one day some time later at BOY Paris, a strange guy was waiting outside the shop in case I turned up. The staff kinda mumbled something at me as I walked in and gestured towards this tall skinny guy in a full-length leather coat. It's one of those strange things but sometimes in life you just sense something about a person, this guy coulda been anybody, probably was going to be somebody one day, maybe a contender, he could have been a young Eminem. He was American and seemed like a massive BOY fan so not to disappoint him I told him I was heading to the Pret a Porter trade show to check out my show stand, which was basically a unit displaying samples of the next seasons collection. So off we went but when we arrived I'd kinda forgotten I was sharing this unit with a German BOY agent, he had a lot of his buyers coming to the show and he spoke, you know like European or whatever. Anyway, it had seemed like a good idea at the time as things do. Unfortunately, I found to my annoyance that he'd only gone and taken all my samples off the rails and shoved them all over the floor in a nearby storage cupboard. The tall American dude picked up on how pissed off I was when the German BOY team, which consisted of one guy and two girls, returned to the show stand. The tall American dude then smacked the Germans really hard and locked all three of them in the cupboard! In their attempt to escape like fucking Harry Houdini they knocked it over and it came crashing down on the ground scaring the shit out of the women in furs holding their toy poodles who then screamed and went running. The outcome of all this was that ironically, I was the one that was banned from showing there ever again, ha ha fucking ha!

Everybody got shot

So, we're speeding down the French AutoRoute on our way towards St. Tropez, I wasn't driving, the Indian was and he had a red Ferrari in his hands, but he wasn't looking at the road, he was looking at me with panic in his eyes.

I loved cars when I was growing up. I used to look into a car showroom in Leicester, peering close to the polished window, and right in front of me there was the car of my dreams that I just couldn't afford. It was a gleaming white MG TD Drop Top. How could I have ever known that one day I would be in a red Ferrari, driving down to my second home in St Tropez. At this exact moment in time though I had bigger concerns as I didn't know if I was going to live or die in the next few seconds the way that the Indian was driving. He was shouting something at me over the revs of the engine, I said, "what's happened John", that was his name; don't know how he got the name of the Indian, but he was a crazy motherfucker. Anyway, he shouted back to me that all of our partner owners of our BOY club in Paris had been shot dead in Miami. He bellowed at me, 'we're the only ones left alive'.

I'm sure you can imagine my pleasure on hearing they were all dead, and even better, the club was now the number one story on the French news as it had been raided and closed by the police for murder, rape and drugs. So, I was thinking it was good thing I didn't get too involved, while shouting at John in the speeding red Ferrari that I didn't give a damn if they were all dead, as the deal he'd set up was fucking useless for me and I was glad they were all in body bags. Seems like they tried to muscle in on clubs in Miami and got shot. Fuck me, it really was like the Wild West back then.

Soho

BOY was fucking rocking, after all this was the fabulous 80s and as I've said before, the streets were literally paved with gold. I was making all the right moves, I couldn't really go wrong, I became the untouchable one, and in fact I was totally on one. It's not such a strange thing to say I couldn't put a foot wrong, especially tracking my history to this point as I hadn't made a single mistake. Don Letts, someone that I regard as a friend, and I have very few, is known for saying Acme was his finest hour. Billy Idol thanks me for mentoring him into Punk and Steve Strange watched me create the Romantics. What was really perverse was I had no idea what I was doing but I realised that neither did anyone else, I just did it better.

Suddenly everyone wanted in on things, I was on fire and the King's Road became the epicentre of 'cool'. Covent Garden was over for me. I was firmly focused on the King's Road and up and down that very road came hundreds of kids, many just wanting to be seen hanging around on the pavement outside BOY. They wanted passers-by to know they were there. Inside the shop you couldn't move and there was a fever in the air. I needed to make my next move. It was time to expand!

A synchronisation took place when the right kind of mind walked into BOY looking to join us. We became a unit, a force that was unstoppable. I don't know why, but it was the only way it ever happened, our policy was no way out, no way back.

Walking into one of my shops or installations, as I prefer to call them, was for some a daunting experience. Crowds would gather outside with French tourists deciding to run the gauntlet and try to get in and out without getting gobbed on. Later on, instead of Punks, there was a much stranger mix of staff working there, like Skinheads with MA1 jackets and camouflage pants. Although they were mostly gay the public found them aggressive looking and were scared of them! By this point BOY had a notorious history, customers would take a deep breath as they walked in, never knowing what or who they might encounter.

My shops were designed to be an adventure, a different world. Like stepping inside my head. I never wanted what people would call a proper shop, I hated shops that were designed simply as money spinners, mine were like theatre, and I chose my staff with that in mind. Obviously, lots of interesting people wanted to work at BOY as it was the hottest place on the planet.

I decided to open in Soho because it was going downhill and the rents were cheap. The trouble was our staff were permanently having to lock themselves in to hide from hordes of marauding football hooligans, that was the way football fans were back then. Then there were the sex tourists looking for girls with signs on the door like 'French Polishing Upstairs' or 'Photographic Model'. Soho was still quite a rough place back then with dodgy looking rain coated characters. There was always at least one mad, hanger on stalking the shops, there was one particular guy called Big Al. If the Soho shopkeepers heard that he was coming to visit they would lock their doors, this guy was over 6 feet tall, a Punk with bleached blonde spiked hair, a leather jacket and Clash pants and he resembled Biff from 'Back to the Future'. He would pick a fight with anyone who even looked at him. He didn't have many friends, he probably killed them all, but I think he liked me and he desperately wanted to be part of the team but my staff weren't having any of it. He was a complete liability, but I really liked him.

Back to the shop. We took a dirty, run-down old sex club with a spanking cinema on Moore Street (I still have the sign for it somewhere) and turned it into a shiny new space with white walls and a white tiled floor, it was pretty spacious, spread out over two floors with enough space to also open an art gallery. I'd begun propelling gay Skinheads into a new arena of photographic art, these images were beautifully extreme, with a certain shock value, which was obviously OK by me. There were also full-size photos adorning the walls of a session with our biggest model Boy George, he was featured with various young male and female models in suggestive poses, shot by legendary photographer and make-up artist Paul

Gobel. I knew the opening night had to be a massive event so we set about inviting as many newspapers, magazines and TV stations as we could think of. We gave the local Police the heads up that we were planning the opening and were expecting press to attend. The surrounding streets were duly cordoned off and crash barriers set up.

We were ready for the big opening and this was a real 'fuck me' moment. The guest list was huge, it included everyone you could think of, the big guns being Madonna, George Michael and of course Boy George. At that time George was our "Poster Boy". We really wanted to open the shop with a big noise, and what better way to achieve this than by asking Boy George to perform at the official opening, which was to be followed by a fashion show at the Limelight. I fully expected him to say no, but he agreed. I wasn't sure if he would turn up or not, it was a crap shoot. He arrived like a mega star with his then boyfriend Michael, and they were both dressed head to toe in fucking BOY! This was one of George's first public outings since his addiction was splashed over the newspapers but he was still every bit the star, the streets were packed – The paparazzi went crazy.

Unfortunately, in my wisdom, or lack of it, I had said "let's put Big Al (remember him?) on the door, he'll love it" and we definitely needed to keep the Soho wanderers out. So Big Al was door manager, however after I'd explained to him the best way to keep people out and he'd helped himself to a few drinks, he ended up stopping almost everyone from coming in! Al was a very old-style Punk, picking fights with everyone! The opening was also marred by a demonstration of locals who didn't want Soho to become a fashion street because they liked it full of dirty book shops and porn shops and I could see their point. It was never gonna remain that way though, which is a pity. At least we turned Soho gay.

At the fashion show afterwards, we launched our 'Red and Black' collection, but I'm a bit hazy about it all as so much was going on. It was held at the Limelight over the road and it ended up in some kind of catwalk orgy............The good old days. As for Soho If I had my time again maybe I wouldn't have opened there as I could see that we were going to change the face of the place completely, but better we did it than the Westminster Council's gentrification plans that came later.

Boy did Soho change! I think that was when we got the title of "the gay label" and I'm not surprised. I've always loved it around there, it's so diverse with every element of life present. It's still full of gay bars, plus Ronnie Scott's Jazz Club, secret private members clubs and even the odd strip joint although many of the old haunts like Madam Jo Jo's and the Marquee club have gone. There was a pub around the corner from BOY called the French House which is still there, it's famous as part of the history of Soho and at the time it was full of anarchists and drunken poets. I went there often just for the atmosphere.

Sometime later after the infamous opening night, when I had just bought a white custom VW GTI, I pulled up outside the shop and who was standing there but Big Al. He looked at me with a certain tension in his eyes, which was his way. So I waved him over and asked if he wanted to cruise round London in my new ride. He looked so happy, I think I noticed a tear in his eye.

Queen Madge

Boy George says that he doesn't get on with Madonna, but that wasn't always the case. On one of his regular visits to the BOY Soho shop, he announced "I'm going to have tea with Madge, and I need to take her some stuff". He then made his way round the two floors of the shop grabbing clothes and throwing them on the counter. Angie and I frantically chucked the clothes into about 10 carrier bags, if not more. We decided that if they really WERE going to be given to Queen Madge, then we wouldn't charge George for a single item – well surely that was going to get us some good publicity? It was the right decision.

When Bob Geldof launched his global fund-raiser for Africa, "Sport Aid" later that same year (1986), a raven-haired Madonna was pictured with a beaming smile as she signed up to run the 10km in New York, wearing a pair of black BOY London cycle shorts, with the label clearly visible on the front. All the money in the world couldn't have bought that kind of publicity.

George also allegedly ran the 10k in London, completely kitted from head to toe in BOY eagle print, but he actually went for breakfast with friends and got a cab to the finish line only running the last few yards! Yet again, priceless publicity for BOY.

MADONNA has got her number for
THE RACE AGAINST TIME on Sunday September 11, 1988

HAVE YOU?

iCL

Carnaby Street

As a top Mod living in Leicester I got down to the big smoke as much as possible for London was the home of the Mods. The pop culture that revealed itself to me as a kid on this famous street nestled close to two of London's greatest landmarks, the statue of Eros and the London Palladium. A small narrow street that was pure gold, so who would've guessed 25 years later I'd open my own shop there. This was the third shop to open in succession after my return to BOY.

After the astronomical success of BOY King's Road, the original flagship store, opening in Carnaby Street was like coming home. I also chose Carnaby Street because it had actually looked pretty much the same in appearance as it had in the 60s and 70s. Many of the same shops had been on the legendary street for far too long though and it was down at heel, dirty and full of traders with no style, who were just there to make a quick buck. They didn't care about the street at all. Now I'm a passionate man and I take pride in everything I do so I decided I was gonna walk in and blow the shit out of this street and bring back some of the old magic.

I began planning my takeover and establishing the coolest looking shop Carnaby Street had witnessed since its heyday. I wasn't prepared to take any prisoners. This was all out war on these cheap looking, tacky shops that had ruined the sacred street and I was determined to bring the old glory back. I often wondered how a Leicester boy like me, with no education or prospects found myself in a position to even contemplate creating my own boutique in the centre of London's West End with all its decades of history.

I had a master plan though and I wanted to design the shop myself in the same way I had ever since I opened PX. Designing interiors was one of my favourite challenges, with no formal training I had managed to gain confidence through nothing but experience, that was part of the territory and the culture I was in back then ...out with the old brigade and in with the new. It was that 'fuck you' attitude that came through everything I did.

I'd come up with this radical idea that the BOY letters for Carnaby Street should be reminiscent of the iconic BOY sign on 153 King's Road only as big as possible so that they covered the entire front shop window. I wanted to utilise our strong logo and make it so big it was fucking impossible to miss. So I had the metal letters made 10 feet high which meant that punters had to peer through them if they wanted to see inside. I had a design in mind for the interior that continued the theme of the giant metal letters. The interior space was black and white, with black metal and glass cabinets which took up the entire floor. There were large black and white images on the walls of models in the latest BOY collections. A black metal structure ran upwards and criss-crossed along the length of the ceiling which contained spot lights and black TV monitors. We were in the MTV age by then and I wanted MTV playing all day long, especially as BOY was featured in so many pop videos at that time. It was an innovative space and it captured the ballsy spirit of BOY perfectly.

I'd thrown out the rule book and with it the old establishment and taken proceedings into my own hands. I was a hot head and just wanted to get things done. It also occurred to me much later in life that all of this styling was more like an art form and I certainly wasn't designing any of it with the general public in mind, in fact I've always hated the general public. I did care about the whole design element though and in turn that appealed to the kind of customers I DID want to attract. Strangely, it turned out it also had an appeal for the man and women on the street! I hadn't really understood back then that this was how architects and conceptual thinkers worked on their designs and visions by not only taking into consideration the actual structure of a building but also the effect it would have on the lives of the people using it. It was an indulgent, independent way of thinking but was so absolutely necessary as I wanted to block out the world around me. I had become intense about art and what I was doing. It occurred to me many years later that what I was creating was actually more like the current pop ups, event spaces and installations that we're accustomed to now.

Of course, the world wasn't ready for me or my design philosophy back then, so I was in my own little bubble. I was always thinking in future terms and looking back I can see that's what my life's work has always been about. The vanguard, the Avant Garde, the artistic rebel, a driving force inside me pushing me on, there was no stopping me. I needed to see this through, whatever 'this' was. Once I've created these projects though, I'm a bit like the director Alfred Hitchcock in as much as I don't go to my own 'screenings'. Once a project is finished I'm off on to the next one however weird or crazy the next one is. I just need to carry on regardless.

Pet Shop Boys

There have been two big acts that are synonymous with BOY, one is Boy George, the other is the Pet Shop Boys. Of course, there were countless others but the Pet Shops Boys connection was one of the most defining moments in the BOY saga. Their big break came with East End Boys and West End Girls, one of the most popular songs and videos ever. It was still the MTV years and the video would be shown over and over. It was and still is a really great video. Even back then I felt that it had a touch of BOY about it, as it represented the London we knew and featured street kids and Skinheads in the same way I had in the BOY catalogues.

The cover of their next single Loves Comes Quickly featured Chris Lowe sporting a BOY cap and it quickly became an iconic Pet Shop Boys image. In the video for their hit Suburbia you actually get a flash of the Love Comes Quickly record cover perched on a mantel piece in a suburban home. There's a picture disk of an interview with the boys where Chris is wearing his cap and that disk is now a collector's item and I have an old press cutting somewhere of both boys wearing the rare BOY cigarette shirt. All these images cleverly and subliminally display their attachment to BOY LONDON.

As it happens I had been walking around London wearing a BOY cap before the two of them even existed as a band, and they'd been coming into the shop for a while to buy from me so it's no secret where the influence for their 'look' came from. Neil Tennant has been on record as saying that he expected the image of the cap to be their 'coming out' moment as it was so gay! You've gotta love it!

I always credit the Pet Shop Boys with being the best promoters of my original BOY label along with Boy George. The fans would flock to my shop to buy anything that had BOY on it and the PSB's were the perfect advert! To this day they're often seen in publicity wearing the BOY cap for press and world tours, it's still the sharpest tool in their wardrobe. It's their signature look as much as it's mine. I'm happy with that as I've always loved their image, music and stage shows. It's unusual for a band to promote a label in the way that they have with BOY. I've always been grateful to them for it and obviously they've bought loads of hats over the years, especially the white ones.

There was a time not long ago when I was sitting in my car with a girl in London's East End by one of my pop-up shops when I spotted the Pet Shop Boys coming up the road in a car. I could tell they were heading to my shop so we watched them as they climbed out of the car and peered around the door wondering if they should go in or not. I think the young male shop boy in heels and a blonde wig who looked about 17 may have put them off. It reminded me of the time back in the day, when Mark Almond of Soft Cell came to my PX shop in Covent Garden but was too fuckin scared to come in!

Hyper Hyper

Hyper Hyper was a huge space on two floors of the world-famous Kensington Market. Owned by nobody's fool, Lauren Gordon who seemed to own half of London's retail areas, including 'Kenny Market' and Chelsea Antiques Market. The idea behind Hyper was to house London's coolest most forward-thinking designers under one roof, with a few of the regular brands to pull in the punters. All the newest young designers were desperate to be a part of it as Hyper really did represent the style and culture of 80's London. It was big, it was brash and there was nothing else like it.

BOY was very well established and respected by now but it took me a year to have a unit that was front of house. We had the first space you came to as you walked in and it was a double unit so we were in pole position. Space wasn't cheap and most of the units weren't big enough to swing a cat! Included in the rent was the use of the Press Office, and any international fashion journalist worth their salt could be found hanging in the basement office nosing through the rails of the new season's samples and the girls from the office would often be found in the units borrowing current stock to loan out to newspapers, magazines, TV and films. BOY was already an internationally well-known clothing brand but having this service on tap was the icing on the cake. Fashion editors didn't have to make a special trip to Chelsea to see our stock, they could see it along with everyone else's in one fell swoop. Perfect! The seminal black and white eagle collection originated in a Hyper Hyper catwalk show, part of London Fashion Week. The fashion press went crazy for it, we had a stand at the accompanying trade show, and that was when it really exploded for us. Buyers from around the globe flocked to the tiny stand and placed their orders – they all wanted a piece of us, and soon we were in leading stores in all the major cities of the world. In New York, where previously BOY could only be sought out in the hip boutiques like Trash and Vaudeville and Patricia Field, suddenly Bloomingdales were devoting whole windows to BOY.

I remember going down to the office where Lauren "Mrs G" Gordon was viewing samples for possible inclusion in their catwalk show. Heated words were exchanged about the eagle motif, as she thought it resembled the Nazi eagle too closely; particularly personal to her as she was Jewish. Somehow, I managed to charm her and she took a chance on the collection which became the most talked about part of that show. I loved fighting and arguing with the press office! The Hyper Hyper runway shows were actually way better than London Fashion Week, they were young, vital and pop.

BOY became stratospheric after that. The BOY baseball cap, already made famous by Chris Lowe from the Pet Shop Boys, was now seen on the head of other pop stars, and film stars. Princess Diana made the trip from Kensington Palace, situated behind Hyper, to buy caps for William and Harry as did 'Lady' Madonna herself!

1986

In 86 BOY went fucking ballistic. We smashed it everywhere, everyone was talking us up. Pop stars were queuing around the block and they all wanted to wear BOY. We had made it to No.1. I'd been in bands where I'd had girls hanging around me even back then so I knew the score, we were just like pop stars only this time the girls were fashion groupies.

One time I took loads of girls to Paris to meet a client, or actually to have fun with the least amount of biz possible, so the client took us to a famous Parisian restaurant in Bastille, the walls of which were covered in huge renaissance paintings. We had hardly been seated when the Garcons came running across to ask for our autographs. They really did think we were Frankie Goes to Hollywood! I guess back then we must have been the only group of people that looked like that on the streets of Paris.

I knew I was on the ladder to success but with no prior experience to fall back on. My story was more like that of a rock star than a fashion designer and I guess it's true I wasn't the archetypal founder of a fashion brand but that's what gave me the edge. I was the new kid on the block, part of the emerging MTV world and no one had been there before me. This was a brave new world and I was the leader.

We didn't care about anything because we were rockin' and I was making a ton of money so I figured it was time to buy my own flat and I liked it around Chelsea, it just felt right. In those days Worlds End wasn't that posh, it was a cool area where artists and smack heads still lived and The Sex Pistols had a den a few streets away. So, I found a great place and it turned out the Thin Lizzy drummer lived upstairs. I was the first person to have satellite dish installed in their rear garden, it was so big it was 4 ft. high like fucking Jodrell Bank! Thin Lizzy's drummer leaned out of his window and shouted, "Wow cool dish maan, far Out". I was ready for MTV and we partied the shit out of that Chelsea flat. I had a Scottish girlfriend, another posh Chelsea bird plus some fashion groupies and a post op trannie, oh and a sex maniac stripper girlfriend from Sheffield. We were a gang and MTV just rocked on and on into the dawn.

Some nights I would drive over Tower Bridge, an icon of London itself and I'd shout out loud "This is all fucking mine!" I couldn't really take it all in though. I would think about how I got there, was it all real? Would I lose it all or just wake up and the whole thing had been in my head? As with all success stories I was feeling high all the time although most of it was self-induced. Not surprisingly I was experiencing anxiety pains. I knew I was carrying the weight of the company, its performance, it's future.

All of a sudden it hit me, the reality that I was isolated and alone despite being on top of the whole fucking world! If the business was going off track only I could fix it, my next collection had to be as good as the last. It was all down to me. The fans didn't care if I was stressed, it wasn't their problem, they kept piling through the door and they just never stopped. On top of all this madness I was living with girls that expected me to provide constant excitement and entertainment, I sometimes think I invented the fashion entourage scene. There were parties that went on for days, there was sex play, fetishism, pansexuality and bisexuality, I was living on the edge. I quickly became addicted to the lifestyle but it was making me ill. I couldn't walk down the road without feeling a sense of paranoia, I thought I was going to explode, my head was hurting and I had to get some help.

It was during my 'living the dream' era in Chelsea that the dark cloud emerged taking all the fun out of life and taking away the lives of people we knew so quickly that we genuinely didn't know who would be next. AIDs was everywhere. Everyday there were news stories of more victims, it was as if everyone we knew was at risk. I cannot explain how I felt, I was checking in the mirror for signs constantly, expecting the worst. London was under attack from the HIV AIDs virus. So, I walked into a private clinic in Chelsea, it was time for a full check-up. The wait for the results only increased my paranoia and anxiety. Somehow, I was in the clear. I figured I was suffering from stress related shit but I was also in

denial about it and there were no therapists as such back then so I was fucked. I was constantly telling myself I didn't deserve the successful life. It felt like I'd been getting away with it and would soon be discovered as a fraud. I was still getting involved in crazy sex games at my Chelsea home but somehow doing mad shit, like changing my car every couple of months, helped me. I remember I sent a girl to a West London car showroom with my credit card in hand and told her to buy me their latest sports coupe. The guilt of it all made me feel good, but for how long? We lost so many close personal friends during that time that later we would be inspired to work with Elton John and his AIDs Foundation.

Driving Cars
(Rants, Raves and Revolutions)

I have always got a thrill from driving the streets late at night, like in the movie Taxi Driver. The later it gets, the more the streets of a big city change. The people of the night, the street walkers, the whores and the hustlers, the prostitutes and the cab drivers pulling up at the Brick Lane bagel shop, which became the centre of London's alternative night scene. It was a place I would to pull up at to chill and it depended on what time of year and what car I was driving as to the reception I received. In other capital cities like Barcelona, Rome or Paris you would be applauded for your style, in London however you're immediately singled out as a poser, or worse, so, if you're in a Porsche with a girl and it's the summertime and you have the top down then you can expect to get a variety of stock comments. I would drive my city by night, to relax and get inspiration and ideas. I just loved driving around late at night with the FM dial set, sounds pulsating through the car. The rules were as follows, you needed a cool car, to be into great music, have style, be comfortable within yourself, have a strong imagination, be wild at heart and absolutely love living the dream. I would never take any of it for granted.

A movie I've always enjoyed is Vanishing Point, about a guy that drove all night and took loads of speed. I would be transfixed by the white line in the centre of road, hearing the sound of the engine, completely in control. There's nothing to beat this feeling, being out alone in the big city, the relationship between you and your automobile, your own private world within the big metropolis. It's one of the best feelings, being the only one out there early in the early morning, pigeons flying overhead, picking out foxes in the beam of the headlights as they scamper behind garbage bins of rubbish. It's a new dawn, it's a new day, as the song goes. Perhaps that's what I've always been doing, forever travelling through time.

MTV years

The hit factory guys Stock, Aitken and Waterman wrote and produced hit after hit after hit. They were a prolific writing team that dominated music in the mid 1980's into the early 90's. There's no denying their huge commercial success and massive appeal for the general public. Like them or hate them they were a major part of the pop industry at the time and had a formula that couldn't be stopped. They presented their artists as clean cut and safe even family friendly, which is about as far away from rock and roll as you can get. Of course, that was a big part of their success and popularity and they fitted neatly into the kind of teenage Smash Hits magazine style of the time.

It was a kind of innocence that had also been around in the 1960's and it was a very British thing. There was something so special about those British pop music moments and PWL stood out as THE sound of the time. There was a touch of genius about this team, they saw raw talent and potential everywhere, even in the office boy Rick Astley and the Australian soap star Kylie Minogue. Although they were the antithesis of both Punk and Prog Rock, ironically two polar opposite genres of music with fans that hated each other anyway, the S.A.W sound was perfect for the MTV years and let's face it bands like Duran Duran hardly wrote fucking high-brow masterpieces either! Its anthemic music and graphics became a quintessential part of the MTV years.

This pop sound fitted in perfectly at BOY. Angie Usher, who was my manager at the time recalls how every S.A.W star that came into the shop wanted to wear BOY clothing. She remembers some of the acts that she personally sold or lent our clothes to for video and photo shoots. The list is endless but includes Bananarama, Kylie, Sinitta, Jason Donovan, Pepsi and Shirley, Samantha Fox, Mandy Smith, The London Boys and Sabrina. Theirs was the music of choice and BOY was the brand of choice. Clubbers were wearing my now famous cycle shorts and tops, BOY T-shirts and caps, dancing the night away to Kylie.

There was no internet back then so obviously no Facebook or Instagram either. We only had music magazines like Smash Hits and Melody Maker and that was how the fans would find out what the pop stars were wearing. They flocked to BOY to buy the same styles as their heroes, if they were lucky they would be in the shop at the same time as the Bananarama girls who would be buying their BOY caps and eagle print stockings!

Just recently I threw a party in Berlin and along came Martin Degville of Sigue Sigue Sputnik. We talked about his hatred of PWL, pretty ironic considering the success of You Spin Me Right Round by his Brummy mates in Dead or Alive. Pete Burns was a die-hard BOY fan of course! PWL were good for BOY and like them or not they were on point. Their music has stood the test of time and is currently going through a big revival. You can't keep a good thing down. The power of pure pop.

Waste of time
(Rants, Raves and Revolutions)

Don't underestimate TV, it has become the new art form. Watching TV may seem like a waste of time but for me it was always art. MTV really kick started the music video, and YouTube followed but neither would never have existed without TV. It was from TV that I started to learn, having missed out on any kind of proper school education. I wanted to see everything, Juke Box Jury, Quatermass, The Brains Trust, Malcolm Muggeridge, the interview with the Sex Pistols, Bowie talking about long hair, Only Fools and Horses and Alf Garnett. There were documentaries on every subject I was ever interested in too, like Francis Bacon, Prog Rock, the band Queen, New York, the art explosion, Punk, Iggy and The Stooges, the history of Rock and Roll, Alex Harvey, T. Rex, Blondie and Patti Smith. Then there were cutting-edge shows like Monty Python, Derek and Clive, Cathy Come Home, So It Goes, Old Grey Whistle Test, Top of The Pops, Joe Orton's Entertaining Mr Sloane, the gay play that shocked the nation, ...SO MUCH STUFF. It literally became my entire fucking education; this was my future. Who else was going to teach me back then? Teachers didn't know Jack shit about any of that stuff. The establishment tried to ban everything cool, everything different - the Mods, the Punks, the Gays, everything that was fun to us just scared the fuck out of them. I watched porn, straight, gay whatever, but it wasn't real. Real came later with cam boys and girls. Now I have become less interested in the sex and more interested in the freedom to be anything.

TV brought us the reality show. I watch shit Big Brother, Ibiza Party Boys and Girls, Blackpool, Newcastle, Hen Parties; because it's all about real people. Then there's the fake people and Z list celebrities who will do anything to get on TV. It's all there and all very watchable for me. It's a social barometer of what's going on out there, mix that with the kind of punters coming into my shops, from Punks to Essex girls and you get a picture of life behind the closed doors of the streets where they live.

Back in the '60's the BBC burned and destroyed the most popular programmes on film, they thought that popular TV was just a fad and that it was much more important to save all the political shit, as that was real history. What a fucking big mistake that was. Now they're cursing that decision because they lost it all. They should have asked me. Lou Reed said he did what he could to get out of school so he could get his real education on the streets, the same goes for me.

On my motorbike, sitting in the empty British streets, combing my hair and talking to chicks with beehives. You didn't need to be a pop star, you needed to be ME. I've seen and done so much, it's a miracle I'm still here. What's it all about, Alfie with Michael Caine, Roger Moore as The Saint, that one in the Welsh village with the big white ball chasing him, that's it, The Prisoner. Fucking amazing. Diana Rigg as Emma Peel in the Avengers wearing her latex cat suits from Atomage in Covent Garden. Both me and Malcolm got inspiration from all that latex; I'm even designing that now in Berlin for a new era of customers. There's a lot wrong with society these days, ... On the one look how far we've come - on the other hand, nothing ever really changes.

A listers

It's already a well-known fact that BOY has always had a long list of celebrity customers, and people watching TV or reading the latest pop magazine, especially in the eighties and nineties would have been aware that their favourite stars had made the trip to the King's Road, Soho, Carnaby Street or Kensington High Street to choose their clothes and accessories.

Many famous faces and celebrities like Boy George and Bananarama would come and flash the cash or credit cards in BOY. In doing so they would always draw crowds of excited fans. Many of those celebs became good friends of BOY, but not all the stars enjoyed that goldfish bowl experience. Tight schedules meant they didn't have the time to shop personally. Instead, the record company management, or a personal assistant would come and choose the next look for them. We could spot them a mile off as they had a different way of buying. Firstly, they entered with a sense of purpose; they KNEW exactly what they were after. Obviously, we were more than happy to help with suggestions as when their celebrity clients wore something brand new from BOY and it was splashed all over MTV or Smash Hits for the world to see it would be fucking great advertising for us!

The journalists and stylists had a different approach again. They would take their time looking through the rails of clothes, and often ask to be shown press samples of the new collections that nobody had seen before. They would then feature our clothes almost weekly in magazines aimed at the teen market like Just Seventeen or the pages of Elle, Vogue and other high-end mags not only in the UK, but internationally. Models and pop stars were often featured wearing BOY in popular newspapers like the Sun, Daily Star and the Daily Mirror and fashion editors from the Times and Telegraph including the infamous Hilary Alexander would browse through the rails looking for pieces for their next editorial.

Here's a who's who of celebs who braved the nonchalance of the BOY staff and actually managed to do their own shopping:

George Michael, Boy George, Diana Ross, Bobby Brown (who happened to come into the shop while his song was playing, and danced around the shop to it), Lenny Henry, Billy Connolly, Anna Piaggi the fashion writer, Mark Knopfler (who bought 2 of everything in the BOY kids collection for his own children), Elton John, Pet Shop Boys, American actress Ali McGraw, Tatum O'Neal, Madonna, Janet Jackson, Bananarama, Pete Burns, Kylie and Dannii Minogue, Anna Sui the fashion designer, Princess Diana, 60's pop icon Sandie Shaw, Cher, amongst many others.

Billy's back

I had known Billy Idol for years, ever since he worked in the shop. Billy was based in Los Angeles by now and we had all heard about his motorbike accident where it was reported that he came close to losing his leg. He was in London playing on the British leg of his sell-out tour, when I got the call to say that Billy wanted 2 pairs of Seditionaries studded boots, one in black and one in white. I rang the shop and asked Angie to go to Billy's hotel when the shop closed to deliver them. So off she went to the Halcyon Hotel in Holland Park, where I told her to ask for "Mr. Rude's suite" – Mr. Rude being the pseudonym Billy was using to stay there. The door opened, and standing in front of Angie, wearing nothing but a bathrobe and a smile was Mr. Rude himself. After the customary hug and kiss on each cheek, Billy offered her a seat, and

explained that his physiotherapist had just left, having given his injured leg a gruelling workout. He then asked her if she wanted to see the scar on his leg and without waiting for her reply, proceeded to turn his calf towards her, showing that most of it was missing. Angie then listened to a lengthy blow by blow account of the accident. Eventually she showed Billy the boots, and made her exit, leaving him to try them on. Mr. Rude? Not really – but when I think of all the girls who would have LOVED to have taken her place, I can't help but smile. It was great when I saw tabloid photos of Billy on his way to the Isle of Wight Festival by ferry in 2015 wearing a BOY T-shirt. Still loyal to his Punk roots way back from the days of the King's Road shop.

Billy has always been a star.

Spain

Apart from Ibiza, which I truly loved back in the days of the summer of love of 87/88 there was also the Spanish mainland and the biggest city of renowned fame was Barcelona. I took an office there, I don't know how I took so many offices, I had an office in Florence, in Paris, in London, in Barcelona and in Casablanca. I'm not sure how I managed to get anything done but anyway here goes, I'm in Barcelona and this was before they redeveloped the city for the Olympics, I loved its rawness back then. Eventually I found a great office, it was a big space and I was sharing it with the prominent French design house with the unpronounceable title of François Maritain Gerbo, or whatever. I also sorted myself out with a cool apartment which was close by. My life there was coming together.

The staff in the office were laughing at me because I'd just bought a brand new black convertible and would always put my seatbelt on, they thought that was hysterical but guess they were still riding around on donkeys! For some reason the huge American fridge in the office was loaded with the chocolate liqueurs, basically chocolates shaped like miniature bottles filled with alcohol, it was the middle of the summer and was around 40 degrees so I loved these ice cold chocolates but the thing is I was a recovering alcoholic and wasn't meant to drink any alcohol but as they were chocolates I thought it was OK until the booze hit me and I ended up off my tits. At night the staff wanted to show me around, take me for dinner, that kinda thing, so we all went out to eat. Now the people from this region of Spain are fkkn crazy about the reputation of their food, they reckon it's far superior to any French food and is in fact the best in the entire world, I challenged them to show me so they did! We entered a dodgy back-street area and they took me through a hole in the wall and we found ourselves in a kitchen with some chefs with long beards and huge fucking knives, we all said hello and were shown into a small but cool eating area with a couple of other foodie guests. This was obviously a hip place that only the chosen few knew about.

First off, they were serving vintage champagne, although obviously that was not on the agenda for me! The fish course arrived and the waiter was happily telling us these were ILLEGALLY fished, there were so many different types of little fish and baby squid I tucked right in. They kept on telling me not to eat too many and not to touch the bread but the bread looked delicious and was hard to resist. Then more food arrived, it was like that French movie Le Grande Bouffe, or whatever, it turned out there were 19 courses to go! Now I'm from Leicestershire where they make pork pies and fine dining involves a chicken masala or the local delicacy of faggots and chips so this was out of this world for me. The main course was brought to us by four guys carrying wooden poles that were supporting a massive paella dish, this was their crowning glory and it was fucking glorious. This was followed by dessert or more like 20 desserts so by now we were into so many courses I'd lost count, not to mention the vintage champagne they were serving to the others every 5 minutes. I understandably thought this had to be it ...but it wasn't. I could see the same four dudes heading towards us in the style of a funeral march. They were carrying another huge dish but this time it was their speciality chocolate mousse. At which point my female companion, who was completely pissed on champers and dressed in her best Westwood, climbed onto the table and announced that there was something she had always wanted to do and promptly threw herself into the mousse and rolled around until she was completely covered in its chocolate decadence. That was a dinner and a half.

I needed to get cracking on pushing BOY in a land that was relatively unfamiliar with Punks and pop culture but needless to say I had a plan. There was this little offshoot South of Barcelona called Sitges, it was a really interesting place with a great style, kind of like the Spanish version of Miami. It was full of bars and snack joints mainly inhabited by gay clubbers in leather so being the entrepreneur that I am I could see that BOY, because of its style and the ethos behind it, could spread from Sitges and move into mainstream Barcelona, much like Soho did for London. So I featured the BOY collection in a boutique there and stuck a huge Andy Warhol BOY poster in the window, we were in business.

Pink flamingos

There's another place I love, a place that nobody knows, a place that I've been to many times with various girls and it's deeply ingrained in my heart and soul. It's where I head to when I need to feel a certain energy, calming and stress free, with wide open spaces, thick set black bulls, elegant white stallions and exotic pink flamingos. It has beautiful white side streets and little cafes and restaurants, an old bull ring and sand dunes. Sometimes I'd book into a small hotel with a balcony on one of the side street and listen to the sound of Spanish guitars and castanets deep into the night. My girls would go out to the fashion boutiques and come back excitedly throwing all the clothes on the bed then do a fashion parade for me as we discussed the cut, shape and fabrics. There is nothing like these moments as the sun has gone down but the warm winds still blow through the room blowing from the Savage land, this place I love is St Martin de la Mare, famous for its gypsy festivals. A place of total inspiration for me, it's situated between Marseille and Perpignan on the route from France heading towards Barcelona. I can live, breathe and feel strong again in this energising place. Sometimes I would drive my car down to the beach at night and put the radio on to catch the sounds floating from my island of love IBIZA.

My mind opened up in this gypsy village and granted me access to my inner self, releasing deep emotions. It's strategically placed for when I'd had enough solitude to escape back to Paris, Nice, Barcelona or Madrid, ready to create again. There's also a town close by which is reminiscent of a city from the 1960's, it's called la Grande Motte. I probably would have named it something different but I would have moved there given a chance and under different circumstances. The problem is you can't live in every place you discover. The buildings and architecture are astounding, it was built at the same time as the Charles de Gaulle airport, maybe designed by the same dudes ....but whatever it totally blew me away.

Turning Japanese

As BOY got increasingly notorious, it started to attract a strange kind of invader. From all over the planet they came, like flies around shit. I didn't like any of them. They seemed to come from behind rocks or up from the drains, I could recognise them from a mile away. Perhaps they were business people, perhaps we were just unlucky. Whatever or whoever they were I spent all my time avoiding them, they were a different species and they were not invited.

One such person managed to get through the net, I guess he didn't fit the identikit and he somehow snuck in under the ropes. In fact, he slipped in so surreptitiously that I didn't notice he was in the fucking ring at all! He was polite, well-spoken and relatively well dressed. Because he was Japanese it threw us off guard and to this day I still don't know what he did or what he was doing. He just appeared, perhaps he'd been talking about setting something up with us or investing in BOY as the one thing he did have was money, shit loads of it! He was throwing it around. He was popular with a lot of people around me, he was young, attractive and had a way about him that was so reassuring that if he told you he had just bought Buckingham Palace you'd almost believe him. So he set up home in Sloane Square, probably the most expensive address in London and when I say home I mean an entire fucking house. Before too long everybody I knew was hanging out round there. I went around once and absolutely hated it, I could see what he was doing, he was systematically buying people using his wealth, charming personality, booze and drugs. I found it most unpleasant but because his place was party central it was popular, as was he, but the question was, why was he buying people? Was it because he was lonely or was there more to it than that? What was his game?

On one occasion he took everyone to the recently opened Joe Allen's restaurant on King's Road, it had a little bridge which you had to walk across to enter. The owner obviously knew him. Another time he took me out one night, just me and him, I agreed to go as I wanted to find out more about him. We went to a new pizza joint that had just opened which was full of hoorays and Chelsea girls who all had triple barrel names and said 'yah' all the fucking time. I hated all of them. He ordered champagne all round and several girls came over to our table and to my shock one of them started undoing the strap on my BOY watch and tried to take it off, I thought fuck me this is gross, how can anybody put up with this shit. It seemed to me that this Japanese guy just wanted to entertain all these free loaders and that was his idea of a good time. Now I'm a person with conflicting points of view or maybe I'd seen so much of life by then that my perspectives had altered considerably. For example, I had a Moroccan partner once who fucked every woman he could at the George V Hotel in Paris just because he wanted to get his own back on French society as the French had always been so racist towards him. So maybe this Japanese guy had made a fortune and had come to London just to see how far he could push things, who knows. One thing is for sure if he had an agenda he was keeping his cards close to his chest and not showing me his next move. As I said previously I can usually spot a wanker but this was a little different. I'm a great chess player but he was moving in another dimension. I wondered if maybe he was working out his next big move but was keeping it under wraps. So, then he started telling me he was close to some kinda golfing champion. I couldn't tell if this was a game, a business venture or just BS. He announced one day that the golfer's wife was coming over to meet us in BOY, OK so now the plot thickens or at least it had potentially become a little clearer.

These meetings can sometimes be real, I'd had this kinda thing happen before when one day a wealthy guy from Dubai turned up in a gold-plated Rolls Royce and said he had brought his daughter to meet us as she wanted to be in the fashion business.

So I guess I thought that anything was possible. It felt a bit weird to me plus I just wasn't that interested. Anyway, one day two Australian women turn up who were something to do with the golfing dude. They swanned up wearing designer outfits, probably Chanel or Louis Vuitton or something. Our Japanese friend took us all for lunch just over the road from BOY where a new cafe in a garden just opened. As we sat there getting into conversation one of the women screamed that her designer bag full of all her money, cards and passport had gone missing, then the other woman shrieks that her bag has disappeared too. I then remembered that a couple of friendly people had

come to our table asking for some directions and whilst we were explaining things to them it would appear that they'd somehow cut away the bags leaving nothing but the straps still hanging there! There's a moral to this story which goes.......don't flash your wealth on the streets of London in order to impress me or you'll end up at the mercy of London scammers when you've only just stepped off the bus from Australia!

Anyway, whether they were anything to do with the golfer dude or not I'll never know but what I do know was the shit soon hit the fan. The truth, the whole truth and nothing but the truth. It all came out about our dear Japanese mate although I can't recall the full diagnosis of who told who what but you can never hold back gossip especially when it's as outrageous as this story. It seemed like the whole of the Australian police force, the FBI and the Australian government was looking for a suave, slick, smooth, methodical, trickster of Japanese origin. He was allegedly selling golf courses to Japanese investors in Australia only there weren't any fucking golf courses. He'd fled Australia with millions and pitched up with the dosh in London but almost as soon as he'd arrived he was gone as if he'd never even existed, and so began a trail of stories rather like this one. Is it just me or is this normal day to day activity in the world of fashion? Who knows....

Reasons to be cheerful

After the Japanese came we suffered an invasion from the rest of the world, obviously the word on the grapevine was that there were opportunities and possibilities to be had at BOY for various cockroaches and crooks. I'd never been in this snake and serpent territory before so it was a completely enlightening experience for me and probably doesn't happen to that many people out there around the globe. It was incredible to watch how it developed and how quickly, I was now a strategic risk.

I didn't really know how to handle this kind of attack and having never had much in the way of education as a result of not bothering to attend school I was kinda out of my depth. As I've said already maybe this was new territory for everyone involved in the Punk scene. Nobody straight could possibly get their heads around the subculture and counterculture that I was working amidst. So, I think these individuals, or vipers were just chancing their arm to see what they could get out of us (if anything) and they all came with their own strategic plans.

A Canadian turned up one Sunday on the tarmac of Heathrow airport, he asked if I'd go along to meet him as he had good news and more for us! He made a point of telling us that he was with his lawyer who he had got out of bed especially for this rushed Sunday morning meeting. So, the long and short of it is that I went along with my accountant to meet this guy who said he was passionate about signing agreements with us for the rights to BOY in Canada. In fact, he even started crying saying that he'd hate for anything to happen to a label as great as BOY and by signing we'd be protecting BOY from unscrupulous merchants and head-hunters. So, he ripped a dollar bill in half and we both signed a half each then off he went back to Canada saying he'd be in touch and so he was. He immediately sent off a payment to us for $40,000 USD but here's the crunch, this time it kind of went in our favour as although the deal didn't happen so there was no BOY Canada, we never heard from him again so we just kept the dosh!

Another moment was when the people at a big chain of UK fashion retailers made their intentions clear that they wanted BOY to be their newest label for their flagship store on Oxford Street. We started getting monthly payments through from them, anything from £5,000 to £8,000 a month. However, my accountant kept asking me if I knew anything about this and I just mumbled 'no'. I didn't want to put my collections into a place like that as I thought it would cheapen our designs. He asked what he should do as we really didn't know why they were sending us these monthly cheques and itemised statements. So, I decided to go there to see what was going on as we definitely had not sent them any stock. I wondered if maybe they'd been sold some fakes and were mistakenly paying us but when I got there they didn't have any items of BOY for sale at all. I didn't give a fuck why or how they made a mistake so we just left it and we got paid again and again.

Tension was building in me and I started to wonder what might happen next, I just had a feeling there was something brewing and I was dead right. I was bang on the money for next in line were the Americans. I arrived at my office one day to find two of the most unlikely candidates for making a move on us that I was ever likely to encounter in a month of Sundays. I literally ignored them I didn't even know who they were waiting for ……and I didn't want to know either. To me they looked like a couple of Mexican gun runners. Anyway, my accountant sheepishly approached me and said, "you'll never guess what" and I replied 'WHAT?!' He proceeded to inform me that the two American guys outside liked my label so much that they wanted to sign an exclusive deal for the whole of the USA. I told him to go and tell them to sling it and FUCK OFF! My account explained quietly, in case they could hear us, that it wasn't that simple. I noticed he was holding a piece of paper in his hand which turned out to be a cheque they'd just written out for $500,000 USD and what's more they'd told him to bank it as it was ours as a goodwill gesture and was not to cover any stock that they would subsequently purchase. "We'll be in touch" they said and from that very moment my life would never be the same again.

What's in a name

Along with BOY's fame and notoriety came the copyists. In 1986, BOY LONDON as it was now known thanks to the Americans, was listed as the third most copied fashion label in the world, behind Chanel and Gucci. Trying to close the fakers down in London using the Trading Standards Department of local borough councils was a pointless waste of time, I spent so much time reporting copies and going through the procedure of identifying them at council offices that in the end we were advised that we would never win the battle. BOY had become a victim of its own success.

I decided to get the name trade-marked but I was told by a prominent trade mark lawyer that it would be impossible as BOY was a generic word, in the same way it would be impossible to TM the words Christ, child or man. Another problem was that these lawyers had never dealt with a Punk ethic before and they'd certainly never come across a character like me either. There I was sitting in their office with spikey hair and wearing bondage, I mean they were never going to take me seriously. There were very few places I could go for advice, so as per usual I felt like an outsider. I know now I was completely wasting my fkkin time and money on lawyers.

Once again, I was too early and the world was not ready for me. Funny thing is I particularly remember the lawyers saying that in order to trade mark the name BOY, it would have to be famous enough to appear in the Oxford English dictionary as a description, something along the lines of, 'BOY, the fashion label or brand', of course, back then there was nothing like Wikipedia. Alternatively, BOY would need to appear in print in guide books next to Buckingham Palace the home of the Queen. Well I got news for you, in the 80s it did appear in London's tourist guides directly above BUCKINGHAM PALACE as one of the places of importance to visit. Unfortunately, not getting an early Trade Mark for BOY meant that throughout the rest of my life I've been fucked over and dogged by relentless copies, fakes and rip offs! How was I gunna know what the world would look like when you fast forward 40 years. If I had successfully Trade Marked BOY back then I could have been a multi trillionaire!

1990s

Soho riot

March 1990 and the Thatcher Government in their wisdom decided to incur a Community Charge or Poll Tax as it became known, an unfair, flat-rate tax charged to each individual person and replacing the household rates previously charged. The newspapers, TV and Radio had all warned that London's West End would be affected on March 31st by an anti-poll tax march which would end up in Trafalgar Square, just up the road to the Soho BOY shop. We had seen all kinds of marches and idiot football hooligans come and go, so didn't think anything out of the ordinary might happen on yet another rainy Saturday.

The day kicked off and a buzz started going around the shops, bars and coffee shops of Old Compton Street that the march was loads bigger than anticipated, but nothing much more than that. Angie and I had arranged to meet for a drink and something to eat after work, so I locked up and we headed to the Garrick Wine bar for red wine and steak frites. As we were tucking into our food a brick went hurtling through one of the nearby restaurant windows. Mayhem followed so we decided to get the fuck out and head home. We passed the shop just to make sure everything was ok. As we walked to Cambridge Circus from Covent Garden we could see cars overturned and small fires that had been started in the road. Shop windows were smashed and fucking alarms were going off everywhere.

I realised that one of those alarms was coming from BOY, our expensive floor to ceiling windows didn't exist anymore! Not only that, but everything from the shop floor had been pilfered. All around people were running and shouting, throwing bricks and missiles and shit. I phoned a glazier to get the window repaired but obviously there was a long waiting list, I guess everyone had had their windows kicked in. We started to clean up and eventually it all quietened down, the rioters went home and our windows were replaced around 4.00 a.m.

The riots meant our Chelsea neighbour Mrs Thatcher was forced to back down over the poll tax. I've never been much for politics but I do enjoy a bit of fucking people power!

St Tropez

Sometimes I would get so restless I would just get in my car and drive. I drove down to the beach in St. Tropez, I just felt the need to get away, hang out around the fashion shops and chill at the beach bars. After a couple of weeks, it was time to leave, so I bundled everyone into the car with their suitcases …….I was parked in the square in St. Tropez, surrounded by French cafes and fashion boutiques, the top was down on the convertible with the beautiful blue sky overhead and as we drove off along the twisting coast road, to my right was the vast blue ocean dotted with little white boats and big expensive yachts. I just kept looking back. Anyway, we got about 50 km's out of town, we were in the middle of nowhere, but I had the urge to pull over. I could hear the groans of the passengers as I they all knew me so well………….
"I can't leave, I said, "I'm going back. Life's too short".

I became addicted to the beach, so I bought a caravan right on the famous beach that would end up meaning so much to me during the fabulous 80's. There was nothing else between me and the sea and I would fall out of bed in the early morning heatwave, the sand was shimmering and the sea and sky were azure blue. I just walked straight in and collapsed into the warm Mediterranean, it was bliss. As I got to know the locals I realised there was a community of mainly British ex pats and some other suspicious looking characters. These were the early days of Brits settling abroad, the 80's version of the Hippies in Ibiza or Crete. It was a great time to be alive. To have a caravan there now you'd have to be a fucking millionaire but back then it was a community made up of beach workers selling swimwear and T-shirts they carried around on long bamboo poles or touting apple and jam donuts.

There were also criminals, guys that had fled London and were wanted by the police. Their mugs had been shown on that crime show on British TV. The main offender was Johnny, who lived there with his girlfriend Sharon, he was the archetypal Essex criminal and was working some scam or other every minute of the day. The first time I met him he rolled up on a motorbike and offered to sell it to me. Another time he asked me if I would go to Spain to pick up a Range Rover and motor boat that he'd left there as he couldn't go himself because there were people looking for him.

Funny thing was, I went to Cardiff to buy a four-wheel drive jeep and during the conversation with this over the top Welsh guy I happened to mention that I had a caravan on the beach in St Tropez. He asked me if I knew a guy called Johnny down there, I said "maybe, why?" he told me that the 'cunt' had ripped him off and taken his eight-berth caravan from him in a dodgy deal that had gone tits up… he wanted to know if was still down there…. I thought, fuck me, Johnny tried to sell me that caravan, I'd better stay on my toes here. Anyway, turns out the guy from Cardiff was a major drug dealer and later that same year when I was watching the news there was a report about a Cardiff man having been shot in a drug deal. I thought, great I can do the deal with Johnny now, coast is clear….

Scam

So, the Americans had muscled their way into my company, greed always finds a way in no matter what. They were now holding the main ticket; all eyes were on them and they were splashing cash everywhere making out that the sky was the limit. They were holding all the cards, they were the movers, the shakers. They had come back to us a number of times after their initial investment of $500k, increasing their orders upwards to one million USD. My accountant was loving it and I was too busy chilling on beaches around the world and hanging out in Mediterranean beach bars in the company of George Michael's pretty boys and throwing sex parties at my Bay of St Tropez home to care.

The Americans created total confusion though with their American licensing deal as BOY America. Then they started to talk about having to protect the label around the world and they brought in their own legal team of trade mark lawyers. They would set up three and four-way conference calls from LA to London and they would further confuse the situation by talking about me and how my salary would increase but they needed to adjust my title from creative director to genius and some other bullshit. They would send lawyers from LA to our office in London armed with maps showing where we had problems in the world with our brand. It was insane. My accountant was good, but he was no match for them and he had completely lost the plot. They had managed to weave a tangled mess of confusion throughout the BOY business.

Then one day my accountant called me up at my place in St Tropez and said we were ruined as the Americans hadn't paid for their biggest order yet and their last cheque had bounced. I was standing on my 60 ft. balcony looking out over the bay and my head was about to explode. I thought, fuck me this time it really IS all over. So, we were now in a massive hole after borrowing a million to produce the order. It wasn't until years later that I realised the Americans probably had a plan all along to steal the BOY label from us. It was such a complex plan that they must have spent years devising it, they were obviously determined to get BOY from us no matter what. We now had no choice but to go bankrupt and of course the Americans were ready to buy the company from us for virtually nothing, the stress of it all was too much for my accountant. The subterfuge was such that in the end nobody knew who was who or what was what. I now think that the Americans were just the puppets and the puppet masters were somewhere in Asia. As if things weren't bad enough I then heard through the grape vine that this Asian dude called Tommy was looking for me and he had a gun. Fucking bastards.

The Americans met their match in the end when another interested party stepped in and offered to rescue the business and get us out of this financial dilemma. Again, it wasn't really what we wanted because as they say, it was out of the frying pan into the fire. I actually loved the fact that they came in, fucked up the Americans and spoilt their game.

BOY and I lived to see another day, albeit one day at a time. Some days I'd wonder if it was all worth it. I think I hit the beach for a while after that. It could have been worse, I could have hit the bottle and gone 'Back to Black'.

The Sting

My first boutique in St Tropez was in a back street, I love back streets as there's always a sense of discovery, to seek out and find an exclusive shop or restaurant, a place only a select few people know about, that only a certain kind of people would frequent. Especially in St Tropez where millionaire's yachts fill the harbour and the rich pass the time by parading their wealth. I was doing what I do best, I was playing my game but with a crooked set of cards. I knew the fashion world went to St Tropez to see and be seen, there were models, rock stars, pop stars, the rich and famous and the jet set in their Lamborghinis. I wanted to be part of this world but I wanted to turn it upside down, do it my way. It wasn't ALL about about laying on the beach under a parasol with young garcon's and topless girls bringing me whatever I wanted. It was also about showing the world my BOY creations. I dressed my gang of London trendsetters in my clothes then let them loose. Everybody was watching, people watching, with one eye on who was wearing the latest designer labels. I wasn't about to let the French and Italians take all the action, I was determined to make the BOY label a strong contender and it was really working. George Michael, and his group of boys, were hanging out at the best beach bar and I'd got to know the owner as well as all the drug dealers down from Paris. I was definitely at the right place at the right time.

St Tropez was awesome in its uniqueness, it was one square mile that contained every fashion brand in the world and the world came to see it. It was nothing like America or England, it had a rebellious attitude mixed with a touch of Bridget Bardot, that's why I loved it. There was loads of sex on the beach, Serge Gainsbourg style, and topless waitresses serving champagne who seemed to know exactly how to behave and exactly what the punters wanted.

My St Tropez habit

I just couldn't kick my St Tropez habit, the lure of the sunshine, beach and Mediterranean was driving me crazy and I just hated being away for too long. After a spell back in London making new collections and opening more stores I was bored again, plus there were more assholes hanging around trying to take over the business so I quit temporarily and decided to head back to the beach. I came up with a plan that was pretty easy to pull together. I'd come up with some great designs for swimsuits, cycling shorts and crop tops, I had a machinist in south London who was working out of her garage making for me and Westwood. She ran up some stock, I loaded up my jeep, got some clothes rails and headed south, straight into the sun. I pitched up at a red striped tent, with some reclining beach chairs and clothes rails right on the beach in St Tropez. I lay back in my deck chair listening to my boom box drinking iced coke and being the king of my own castle. The plan was mad but it fucking worked, I was mobbed. I needed more sales assistants.

It was mid 90's, the Spice Girls were around, Princess Diana was on a huge white yacht out in St Tropez bay, and I'd finally opened a boutique which this time was next to the famous night club Papagayo. It was just off the port and there was a cool bar opposite that had a football machine outside that served tequila shots all day and night. It was still in a bad boy part of town, just enough to give it that fuck off flavor I always loved. I was selling tons of Spice Girls merchandise along with BOY clothing, BOY watches, swimwear and club wear. I decided to stay open 24 hours or at the very least be the last one to close. We had customers from all over the world, Dutch, Swedish, American and Australian but the best customers were without doubt the Italians. Funny thing is the English were the worst. The Italian's almost understood BOY as they were into street couture which was my thing. It's what I've always done best. The Italians would shop until they dropped, turning up at the boutique after midnight, changing in the window, stripping naked to

show off their tattoos before heading out to a club. It was hard to get a store in a good location in St Tropez because the French would try to block anyone new from moving in. It's a mafia type thing….

I was making headlines in the town, getting known, being invited to lunch by club owners, it was a kind of French, I scratch your back you scratch mine, kind of thing. The owner of Papas, the club next to BOY, invited me for lunch in the garden area of the bar, I could see Rod Stewart eating at one of the tables across from us. Anyway, the owner suggested we do something together like a fashion party night to promote the club, I agreed and asked him what he needed, he said great looking girls and runway models. In return my girls could party for free every night! I said, 'OK it's a deal'. Little did I know what trouble I was getting into. From then on, I was always looking for the girls and trying to round them up so that they could open the BOY boutique the next day, but they were still mashed and drunk from all the free drinks they'd had the night before. It did also have its compensations……

After Papa put a spectacular show called Red London Bus Stop, the whole of St Tropez was in on it and every other club in town wanted a show. Gay, straight, celebrities, they all wanted in on the act and I was now booking models to keep up with demand. This meant that my apartment was filling up with girls, a problem I was all too happy to have forced upon me! There was one girl at that time that resembled one of the Spice Girls, the red headed one. She had become part of our entourage, although she said she hated me she decided to fuck me anyway as there was another girl I was getting closer to and she wasn't having any of it. So the red head and me would get up to some shit together and cause a scene wherever we went. She loved being the centre of attention and I loved helping her achieve it.

When back in London I had done a favour for a well-known Dominatrix, funny thing is I can't remember what……. Anyway, her thank you present to me was to send two of her best girls on holiday to my apartment in St Tropez. Unfortunately, they encountered a small problem on arrival with the French customs officers. When asked to open their cases, everything came

tumbling out. There were neck harnesses, chain leads, butt plugs, dildos of all colours and sizes, vibrators and various other dominatrix equipment. These girls were sent to please at all costs and they made that known to me. Needless to say, after the second night of pure debauchery I was in love.

I took them both shopping in Cannes the next day as they wanted to buy Louis Vuitton and Chanel bags and luggage. The service at these stores was amazing with staff waiting on them hand and foot and seemingly appearing from everywhere. The girls whispered to me…. 'If they only knew who this platinum credit card belongs to it would bring down the entire British government!'

Later Boy George came to stay at my apartment when he was visiting St Tropez to take part in a catwalk beach event I was putting on at Aqua, the gay boys beach. I set off to pick up George from Nice airport with his DJ friend Jeremy Healy from Haysi Fantayzee. Jeremy had recently worked with George on the music and video for No Clause 28. I picked them up in my gleaming white BMW with the top down and we were singing along to the new record by Black as we made our way along the same coast road where Princess Grace of Monaco had died in a car crash when she hit a retaining wall, veered off the edge of the road and her car hurtled down the cliff.

On our way we came to a popular small French seaside resort and I decided to drive right through the centre of town. We spotted a typical French looking boutique selling swimwear, shorts, suncreams and beach towels, some of which had amazing acid house designs on them, so we jumped out and bought the whole lot. We jumped back in the car and motored on towards St Tropez calling into my apartment to off load their luggage and to give George time to get ready. George was in typical Boy George mood and anyone that knows him will know exactly what that means. We didn't get down to the beach until late because George was of course being George and waiting there already was the crew, some extras and a helicopter that had flown in the Nice Matin news production team. The whole event was filmed in one take. We went into town to watch George on the news the next day when ironically both George and

...emy were asked to leave the local supermarket
...not wearing shirts or some French shit like that.
...returned to my apartment, got ready and headed
...onto the streets of St Tropez. George decided
...that night he was gunna go out in full on Boy
...rge mode completely dressed in BOY just to see
...t would happen. What happened was the whole
...came out to see him, they were clapping and

...shouting from restaurants, bars and shops, eve...
wanted a piece of the Boy's attention. The next
he went out as himself, just plain ole George ar...
of course nothing happened at all, nobody knev...
he was or recognised him. I remember thinking
powerful the BOY image was when teamed up v...
British icon, the one and only BOY GEORGE!

George Michael at the Val Rouge beach

George Michael was often in St Tropez. The first time we saw him was in the Byblos Hotel pool, he was with a Japanese girl and in the paper the following day it was reported that she was his latest girlfriend, but one of our crowd had blurted out publicly that he was gay.

It's funny how he had managed to cover it up but it was easier back then. Anyway, the Wham Rap single had just been released and a lot of people thought they were an American band. I think it was the young guns thing or maybe the Wham Rap video where they were wearing Choose Life T-shirts. The next time George turned up in St Tropez he'd discovered Le Val Rouge beach bar and restaurant where me and the BOY posse were well known and would often hang out. The only good thing the fuckin Indian who sold us out ever did was introduce me to the owner of Le Val Rouge beach bar, it was hard to get a spot there as you were expected to be 'someone'. George Michael was free to hang out at the bar with his cute Italian boyfriends without being photographed by the Paps.

Another regular occurrence at Le Val Rouge beach bar was when a DJ from Le Palace club would turn up after luncheon and spin records all afternoon. In the usual French mode, the girls would climb on the tables and dance with roses between their teeth and show off their asses! Occasionally the 'sex police' would visit the bar, they were two topless girls wearing what looked like military police caps, they had cameras slung around their necks and would photograph people in the bar then invite them to party at the Lamborghini villa overlooking the Mediterranean. We would be on that list and we'd rock up to the party where David Bowie tunes would be blasting out around the huge swimming pool, sex and drugs were going on everywhere and there was even a poodle surfing across the pool with an outboard motor attached to his board! Fortunately, I was one of the first on the block to get a Panasonic camera and I used it to video the whole thing, in fact I videoed the whole of the fucking 80's so I know it's all true.

The bodyguard

I was thinking about my life and everything that's happened and how certain things have had a habit of catching up with me. I try hard to not to let them in because I never realised how certain moments would affect me forever. I was just watching the movie The Bodyguard for the first time recently and I remembered how I'd ignored films like that at the time and how I assumed that life would just carry on forever, whether that was my life or anyone else's, the thing is it doesn't.

Whitney haunts me always, I remember her biggest song 'I Wanna Dance With Somebody', it played and played so much it drove me crazy! Every dancer in the video was wearing a top with the black BOY eagle on a plain white background which was amazing publicity for BOY. It was a great song and one of her best, it played along the boardwalk in St Tropez all summer long. That particular time left a lasting image of my life back then. Once there were half a dozen girls living in my apartment and the occasional beautiful boy, I threw tons of parties, I was in love with everything around me - I just didn't know it at the time. I was so shocked and upset when Whitney died. It was the same with others that have died around me like the black model Sam who was wearing BOY designs when he jumped off a Californian bridge.

BOYS BOYS BOYS

BOYS BOYS BOYS was sung by the Italian girl Sabrina. In the video she's in the swimming pool with her tits bobbing up and down and the fucking Italians lived it and loved it. It was part of their culture, like Botticelli meets sex, sea and sun. So, there I was in yet another city. I began working in Italy around 2004 with Fiorucci as I liked him and his style very much and because he had decided he wanted to open a BOY store in Italy. That is to say he wanted to make a small replica of my BOY store within his larger flagship store in Milano. That was the way he worked. Like me, he loved art and design and the spirit of things. He was an expert at promoting new ideas and recreating old ones. He was a self-confessed guru of life and style, much like me, so we got along.

After my collaboration with Fiorucci I returned to Italy a few times, I loved the drive from Menton in the South of France. Back then, about half way through the tunnel crossing from France to Italy the character of the tunnel changed from a beautiful smooth white road into hell with muddy walls, no proper lighting and only rags on fire in bins along the tunnel. It was like a Fellini movie, it was absolutely adorable. I love Italy for its madness, its baby Fiat cars, its fast red sports cars, the dodgy guys in petrol stations with a dozen fake watches up their arms that will happily sell you anything you want and the little shop behind the petrol pumps that only serve espresso café, blood red orange juice and toasties, which are Parma ham and cheese toasted sandwiches… fkkn ace.

Nothing is easy, it never is

I got everything I wanted, but it wasn't easy. I had to make constant changes and decisions about my journey through life because I would rather die than do it the wrong way. I guess I was a pioneer of sorts, and there were always those forks in the road saying, "Go this way - no, go that way". They say there is another planet up there somewhere that is exactly the same as Earth but the exact opposite, so every decision we have ever made, the opposite will have been made there.

If I had been born a rich kid it would have been so easy to make decisions, because you couldn't go wrong, you always had your back covered. But I had to do it the hard way, and that's what makes your story your own personal movie, the wallpaper of your life. Plus, I never liked the rich too much, they generally have no soul and just buy expensive shit because they think it's cool. It isn't cool, it's flashy and it takes no creative thinking at all to go into a store and buy shit like a Porsche, a duplex in New York or whatever. I couldn't do that, my parents would buy me clothes in the sales, or stuff at knockdown prices that the shop couldn't sell. Once they bought me a green Norfolk jacket. I hated it, and I was embarrassed to go out wearing it, but now I love stuff like that. I started to learn quickly and learn a lot. Girls liked you if you were different, if you had style, you can't buy style. They could tell you had that certain "something" that can't be learnt from books.

I was a street kid. John Lydon and Sid Vicious were street kids. I didn't go to art school or design college, I just made it up as I went along but that seemed to attract people to me. I seemed to draw them in, and they wanted to know more. I don't know what it was, maybe my curiosity about everything was intriguing to them. It turns out I wasn't normal. I discovered that Bertolucci, the film director used to say he wanted to find the dark side of his leading ladies as it was a side that was always present, it was just a matter of discovering it. I found myself in many situations like that through my life; I guess we are like artists or poets like a young Bob Dylan sitting on a bed in some bohemian apartment with a group of girls around him. What a great image that is. So I learned quickly that something else that's attractive is a "couldn't give a fuck" attitude, it's all about how you live, the music you listen to, the way you talk and act. It's the opposite of how most of our parents lived. It's not giving a shit about the future but being radical and forward thinking at the same time. I would often go out to buy the most current thing I could think of at the right price. I would buy a car or live in an area that was really down but I could see that it had something. It was talking to me. Everything I bought seemed to rocket in value and everything I did became the next trend.

I wanted everything and I got it, but that's a long story... shit I just remembered I'm actually meant to be writing a long fucking story....... Anyway, I've had fast girls, fast cars, a fast life and I've been living the dream but I Did it My Way (thanks Sid). I don't know how I did it coz I was never in one place long enough. One minute I was in London town, the next somewhere else, like a beach in Italy or Cannes or clubbing in Ibiza. Driving around in fast cars with girls throwing their underwear out of the car window. What more could a boy want. I tell you it wasn't easy. I didn't stick to the script. When things were going well I would deliberately fuck it up. When I was on the good side of things like Ibiza with its cool clubs, beaches, stilt walking girls with fans, I wanted to be on the bad side with the hundreds of girls over from Manchester or Hull living it large in a copy of a northern boozer. I've always wanted to be somewhere else other than the place I was. I was constantly on the edge of fucking it all up. I was never in one place long enough to really build up a business, truth is I didn't like business. I was the instigator of many things but I also loved the anarchy and disorder. I would put myself in impossible positions, maybe because I'd seen so many 'where are they now' stories, on past stars like George Best. I didn't want the wife, house and kids or to be middle class, so I decided better to say, 'fuck it', live my life and see what happens.

In recent years I've had people, some almost unknown to me, getting in touch to tell me how I had influenced their lives ...that's fukkin mad isn't it? I was talking to an Australian girl recently and I asked her if by chance she'd heard of a girl I knew years ago who'd moved back to Australia. I joked about my comment as I aware that out of a population of millions I knew it was unlikely, so yeah, a pretty stupid question. She came right back though saying sure, she knew her, she was now an artist in Australia and she'd talked about meeting me and how it had changed her life. I've also had other girls and boys thank me for giving them some hope and a chance to turn their life around. That's another reason for writing this book, it's not for my ego, or to get back at anyone, it's about the importance of believing in oneself....

Alive

My return to London in the mid 90s was necessary although I didn't really want to commit to anything in particular, I just needed to get back on track. I knew I'd fucked up with BOY as I'd spent too much time hanging out with girls and boys from Ibiza to St Tropez and had taken my eye off the ball. Who could blame me though as everything I had done up to this point had seemed to be right at the time and had kept me challenged. I had a feeling that something was kicking off in London that I could hang my hat on and give myself some street cred. It was towards the late 90s and music was changing again, Absolute Radio and garage gave me a new thrill. London's East End had opened up new possibilities that I could see might turn out to be my saviour and drive me forwards again. I didn't think about BOY too much at that point, I was just doing what I do best and figuring out if I could get this right, hoping that maybe the whole world would fall into my hands again.

So, I was back on it once more and we moved our work studios from opposite BOY on King's Road to further down towards Worlds End and turned the new place into our design headquarters as well as a place to sample new creations. The new work studio was the place from which we created our Smiley collection and later my pinstripe suits and BOY ROX the WORLD patches and badges that we put on

bombers. These collections definitely hit the spot and were a great success. Then one day Baby Jane turned up. She desperately wanted to be involved, she was 13 going on 18 and her mother came with her on most visits. We built our 90's collection around her and called it the Baby Jane collection. It featured some firsts as we were the first fashion company to put out collections called DOPE, SAFE, FUNKY FRESH, ATTITUDE, BRAVE BOY, 24K GOLD, CAMO, COPY AND DIE. These included sports cut joggers, shorts, jackets and bum bags, it was one of my favourite collections. I personally wore it for years but I'd made a mistake by being too far ahead of the game again. Tommy Hilfiger picked up the look five years later and it became massive. When I put the collection down the runway the stupid fucking NYC buyers walked out saying "these are street people, like black and stuff, we get mugged by people who look like that, how can this be fashion?"

Despite the idiot Americans I was back on top again, creating a whole new vision of London with a whole new generation and breed of avid followers to keep my legend alive for just one more day. After what felt like only hours and minutes later the 'stars' were coming out and into my life, it was a new beginning and it started me up all over again. I am Alive.

I'm ravin I'm ravin

It was the 90's and rave culture was big and wasn't going away anytime soon. I was living in Worlds End, Chelsea and me and the posse would stay up all Saturday night. Sometimes we watched the Hit Man and Her, it was a crazy TV show that didn't quite pull it off but that's actually what was good about it. It had a Britishness, it wasn't slick, for a start it had Pete Waterman as a presenter so it was never going to be that cool. It had a certain Northern charm though which I actually liked and some of the music was fierce and club orientated, after all it was about clubbing and the whole show was devoted to a different club each week. They filmed the whole show in a Northern club which gave it some edge and there was quite a lot of BOY clothing worn by the kids on the dance floor. Incredibly it didn't come on the box until 1.00am, this was Britain on a roll with rave culture. So, I would have the TV on and maybe the radio too on some illegal pirate station listening out for shouts going on after midnight. Sometimes we'd hear there was a movement happening around the M3 or wherever, a meet up at Chiswick or maybe a filling station in Kingston where an official meet would be going on. We'd head out of Chelsea and there'd be loads of cars on the road we'd all meet up at the filling station to be told that there was a rave in Reading. There would be hundreds of cars there and one time it turned into a riot rather than a Rave!

It all happened so quick and the police were nowhere to be seen. I had a black car that was bullet proof, and as I circled the petrol station some ravers in oversized hoodies were trying to peer in through my car windows. They were excited because they'd heard that the E's had arrived. We sped off to catch up with the others in the main herd of cars. We saw one or two cars on fire and abandoned on the side of the road, probably nicked. The mood was starting to get stoked up. It was announced on the radio that the herd was moving towards Bristol to a field in some village in the middle of nowhere. We could see the strobes lighting up the countryside and could feel the bass thumping in the air.

So we were 'following the herd' and we came across this field, it wasn't Glastonbury that's for sure but we were in the womb of British rave culture well before the plod had sussed out what was going on. Don't you just love it when you're the first, you've seen it first, done it first, I'm always first. Things were heavy around the entrance, it looked like they were expecting trouble. I noticed what looked like an automatic rifle under one of the organisers coats, these guys sounded like Mancunians to me and maybe they were looking for other gangs trying to take over their patch. Don't you just love it when it's like this, no lightweights around this place… It was what I call Xtreme nightclubbing.

The night got out of hand and eventually the Jam Sandwiches (cop cars) arrived and closed the rave down. We ended up sleeping in a layby at 5.00am only to get a tap on the window of the car from a cop telling me I couldn't park there. "yes officer"

The road to Morocco

Things were going really well, we were dressing loads of celebrities but I was beginning to get bored with the same old pop stars, fashion set and fetish parties. So looking at my two 4x4 red Jeeps with BOY LONDON emblazoned on the back-spare wheel, I was ready for something different and we'd had this Moroccan partner for a short time. The staff at BOY hated him, he would suggest the girls pose in the BOY shop window and do robot dancing, my girls just stared at him in that 'what the fuck' and 'who the fuck' are you way. Anyway, he had a big contact to manufacture stuff in Casablanca, at the time that part of the world was producing all the Paris fashion brands so I thought about it for a bit and decided to go for a long drive, all the way to North Africa! It just hit me that I needed to go when I woke up on yet another dull day in London, I'd always loved the 1940s movie Casablanca plus I wanted a taste of the desert like Lawrence of Arabia and I had two, four-wheel drive Jeeps just parked up doing nothing except the occasion drive around Chelsea.

So I set off after choosing the fittest Jeep I had, I packed it with necessary items for a couple of thousand-kilometres desert safari. Stuff like Maltesers, Kit Kats and diet Coke, hedonistic! I was heading through Paris down to Espana, sleeping now and then in the odd lay-by. Grabbing power sleeps is great, I love to wake up not sure where I am or even who am I. Now steaming through Barcelona with the noise of the wind rushing by and the clouds gradually disappearing, time to start wearing T-shirts, arm out the window. Sun out, things are as good as they're gonna get. I hit the port at the bottom of Spain near Gibraltar. Got ripped off at the port typical scammer style, which is funny because the police were parked right near me, come to think of it they were probably in on the scam and it went like this. A guy came up to my car as I was queuing and moving down the line towards the boat over to north Africa, the guy asked for my ticket so I showed him and he took it and disappeared forever. Maybe I should have stayed in London.

I bought a new ticket and boarded the boat where I found myself surrounded by a rally raid including back up trucks, ambulances and a helicopter. Desert rallies had become popular and I could dig that, in fact I quite fancied the idea. So, these rally dudes were walking around the deck admiring my American Jeep and asking if I was in the raid party, I told them I was just driving to my new office in Casablanca and they just stared at me. After a long pause they asked where my navigator co-pilot was, I stared at them, paused, then I said I was just on my own. They looked confused and pointed out that I was in North Africa and that it was kind of dangerous. So here are a few tips for anyone stupid enough to follow in my footsteps. Don't drive in Africa in the middle of the night. Watch out for trucks pulling out in front of you without any warning because African drivers drive with God. Watch out for large animals on the road either dead or alive and charging right fucking at you. Watch out for sleazy, slimy police every 30 clicks sitting in army jeeps with their caps on the back of their heads just waiting to pounce on unsuspecting motorists. They stop you and whilst smiling, hold out their hand for money, so also remember, only carry small change on all trips. If you happen to be passing through villages with locals wearing hooded blanket coats with goats and shit all over the streets beware of the one arm man jumping on the boot of your Jeep shouting Manchester United, it's likely to be a Moroccan footy fan! If the one armed footy fan then tells you to give him your passport so that he can help to get you through the customs border, don't be too quick to tell him to piss off! As I was nearing the border it was becoming clear that it was gonna be a long wait for my turn to officially cross into North Africa. I was beginning to feel a bit anxious. Eventually my turn came and the whole process was pretty primitive. The officials were shouting for me to show them my papers and of course I had the wrong papers or rather no papers which when attempting to get through the North African border is definitely not a great situation to be in. In fact, it was so 'not great' that the border guards started jumping up and down getting pretty aggressive. How was I to know that I needed special documents to take a car into Africa.

Anyway, they kicked me around a bit then banged me up behind bars in the local prison. Next thing I knew the fucking guy with one arm turned up, like some scene from the movie the Fugitive, he came to my cell and reminded me that he'd told me to give him my passport so that he could get me through customs. Turned out that if I didn't fancy spending any more time in a Moroccan jail I was gonna have to pay, or should I say bribe, each of the five customs officers starting with the chief and going on down through the ranks! So I paid up and I got outta jail! Maybe I really should have stayed in London. Anyway, I was free but if it hadn't been for the guy with one arm I could still be there to this day. I'm sure there's a moral in there somewhere but fuck knows what it is.

I was back on the road and heading for Casablanca, which by the way is nothing like the movie. I'm now following the instructions on a bit of paper that I'd been given back in London. I was heading for a hotel in the centre of the city called the Hyatt Regency and remarkably I found it. On pulling up outside the grand entrance and being greeted by porters I could sense I was being stared at. I started to think it could be to do with the Jeep that was covered in dust and feathers and shit with half an antelope attached to the front bull bars. Or it could have been my appearance as I looked like an extra from Raiders of the Lost Ark with my bucket hat, oversized long T-shirt, ripped denim shorts, mirrored shades and sneakers. I mean I wasn't to know what the dress code was, nor did I know that the Moroccan Mo' Fo' was gunna book me in the plushest 5-star hotel in Casablanca. I walked through the lobby which was like St Pancras station only bigger and everyone else was wearing a suit, even the girls. I was led to my room and the porter opened the door and I went inside. I looked around and noticed everything was gold plated and I was about 22 stories up. I freaked out and rang my Moroccan host, I got his voice mail so I left a message shouting "I'm a celebrity get me out of here".

Eventually he called me back and asked what the problem was. They'd obviously booked me into the newest and most beautiful western style hotel, but it wasn't really my thing so being careful not to upset them, as they obviously wanted to impress me, I asked them if they had anything nearer the sea. Like the genie in the magic lamp they moved me into a hotel right on the beach with a beautiful swimming pool surrounded by reclining pool chairs and furthermore there were young handsome waiters who were there to deliver me bowls of fruit all afternoon. I would have been quite happy to be booked in to this place forever. I felt like I was being massaged by the sea winds but in fact it was one of the very fit pool boys who was attending to my every need. Oh the simple life! People think I always run away and maybe I do but I'm also running ahead on my journey of life, I couldn't have created the things I have without these detours and distractions. Yves Saint Laurent went to Morocco to find himself, he ended up buying a fuck off house there and built an amazing, psychedelic blue garden. I could see the attraction.

Now I had to get down to doing some work. It was great to work with factories that could design and print the cloth while you waited, you'd only been able to do that in America back then. We worked hard all week and at the weekend, to relax, I would go with my hosts and friends to the desert and to Marrakech in a convoy of four-wheel drive Jeeps. We'd eat, rest, gamble and play at Mamounia with its £1,000 a night rooms, then we'd hang out until morning at a disco below the hotel, where white, stretched four-wheel drive Jeeps would pull up and out would step Sheiks dressed in their white and gold robes, they would walk past the 20 or so white stallions that were protecting the entrance with mounted riders who sat silently with curved swords at the ready. 'And above us only sky', a sky full of stars.

Elton John

Elton John was a fan of BOY from around the time of my return to BOY after the PX days. Along with the Pet Shop Boys, Elton has always loved to wear hats. He would often stop by BOY and check out our latest creations. Sometimes he would fancy a brand-new hat sample that we only had on display in the window and Angie would tell him to stop by in a week so that she could re-dress the window display and have the hat ready, waiting for him. He wore one of the original BOY caps I made in black and gold, for a performance on Top of the Pops of his first ever number one single, Sacrifice.

Then the AIDS epidemic hit. We'd lost a lot of people, it was like the third world war. Everybody was nervous and uneasy. We didn't know how it was contracted or who'd already got it. It was like Russian roulette and our friends were dropping like flies. One of the first to die was John Crancher a fashion designer with a high-end couture label called L'Anarchy. He was a personal friend and at the time we were designing a collection called No Future together. I watched him losing his grip on life as we drove around London together. It was fucking grim. If we called into the local gay bar full of YMCA clones, with back pocket hankies and all that, you know the type, the mood was pensive, nobody knew what was going on. This was not a great time to be gay. Because we knew Elton John well at this point and he was a big fan of BOY and good customer I decided to see if we could get together with him and help. We'd just taken a shop in Spitalfields Market, so we set about opening an office in the basement.

Once the new office was sorted we made it available to Elton, I suppose looking back we should have made it all more legal and legitimate but these were still the early, naive days of London in a way, especially in the East End and that's how I always worked duckin' and diving. Angie and I worked closely with Elton to raise money for his newly set up Elton John AIDS Foundation. We brought in some of our wealthy Japanese clients and Elton was able to enlist Princess Diana who was always a massive fan of his. Elton opened a store in order to sell off some of his huge collection of clothing, it was an immediate success and he raised thousands of pounds for his foundation. As Angie had helped him manage the whole venture she and I were able to get first pickings of some of the best pieces before they went on general sale. I bought myself one of Elton's studded leather jackets, I still have it……. We made a collection of BOY watches for Elton to help raise money for the foundation. He's done a lot of good with the foundation over the decades, not only raising money but also awareness of what was at that time a death sentence for many.

LALA London

It was so surreal around Spitalfields back then, there was nothing going on but the old East End life, it hadn't moved on and was still the way it had been for decades before. The area was made up of wholesale shops and empty pubs, they were always empty, deserted pubs in areas that had previously been fruit and veg or meat markets. Same as it was when I opened the very first shop in Covent Garden, they all had 24-hour licences but no customers. So, on the first day in the office in Spitalfields I took a walk around the area and found a pub opposite, I think it was called The Golden Heart. The door was open and it was dark inside, Country and Western music was playing on the Jukebox and a small dog tried to bite me on my way in, there was an old geezer leaning on the bar and a lone Skinhead. it was a stone's throw from the church where Jack the Ripper had hung out and later they would run night time guided tours of the famous Ripper streets. The Golden Heart pub and Sandra the owner would eventually become wealthy as the pub I had landed in and begun to frequent with my LaLa London gang would soon became a real hot spot, with the likes of Tracey Emin, Kate Moss, Pete Doherty and half the fucking brat pack of London drinking there! I've begun to really dislike my journey through regeneration and gentrification, back then this was a very real part of London's East End and for me the developers have destroyed the Brick Lane area completely.

I had also taken a residence in nearby Fashion Street, which was ironically one of the least fashionable streets at the time but I loved it. Rents in Spitalfields Market were on the floor and businesses were only just nervously moving in to the area one by one. Gilbert and George would walk by every day to go to a little restaurant next door, they were famous for going to the same restaurant each day and refused to eat at home as they disagreed with washing up, I get that! So, we set up shop in Spitalfields and called it LALA London. Soon enough it was the place to be, we even dressed The Spice Girls there!

Nobody took me seriously back then even though I was carving and creating a pathway through the whole of London turning everywhere into gold. At that time, I hadn't realised that what I'd been doing all along, since moving to London was opening up new low rent areas in derelict parts of London, then creating my magic. These areas always ended up turning into the most high-trend parts of London.

It came to my attention that there was one person who got me, he could see I had something, that I could read the future and he wanted me. He sent out a message through the grapevine and while I was doing a trade show in Manchester with the BOY jeans collection, I was approached by several salesmen all suggesting I go see some guy they knew in London as it would be worth my while. So, I went to meet him, turned out this guy was a big deal and owned swathes of Oxford Street. In the most ridiculous meeting I've ever been invited to, we sat at opposite ends of a 40 ft. long table. He was sitting between two accountants who kept lighting his cigars, he then announced that he would offer me millions for my BOY label, fuck me that was a lot of dosh back then! But there was to be no selling out….

Spice Girls

One day I took a call from Elton John in a panic because the sponsor for a big East 17 gig had pulled out and left everyone in the shit. I really liked East 17 and Elton said the band would do a special edition BOY watch for me as a thank you for stepping in at such short notice. So, BOY London was now East 17's new sponsor but there really wasn't very much time left for me to develop an amazing presentation but it needed to be something fucking amazing bearing in mind this gig was to be held at Wembley stadium and was the bands biggest gig to date.

So, I set to it and worked with my video production team to create the opening visuals that would read "BOY LONDON presents East 17 at WEMBLEY STADIUM'. It was definitely a rush job but we had just enough time to film a short video which was projected behind the band as the concert opened up. Of course, I was there that evening and it was fkkn nuts! There were girls screaming, standing on the seats and running around wearing little crop tops and loads of camouflage clothing and all sorts.

The next day after this momentous event, a stretch limo pulled up outside my BOY office and out spilled The Spice Girls. They were exactly as they are in that video for their fabulous first single and No1 hit Wannabe, I loved that song and the video, I'm pretty sure it was at the top of the chart for weeks! FUCKING GIRL POWER!

Of course, they hadn't even released it at this point, but they had been at the gig the night before and they'd come along to my office to introduce themselves. They took over the entire office and said "hi, we're the Spice Girls and we want BOY LONDON to represent us as we're gunna be really famous". I remember making some cool clothes for them and I thought they were amazing but as for managing a gang of girls in a band, I'd already done the whole Billy Idol thing and to be honest I knew they would do my head in. Not to mention you would have needed a degree in psychiatry to manage that lot!

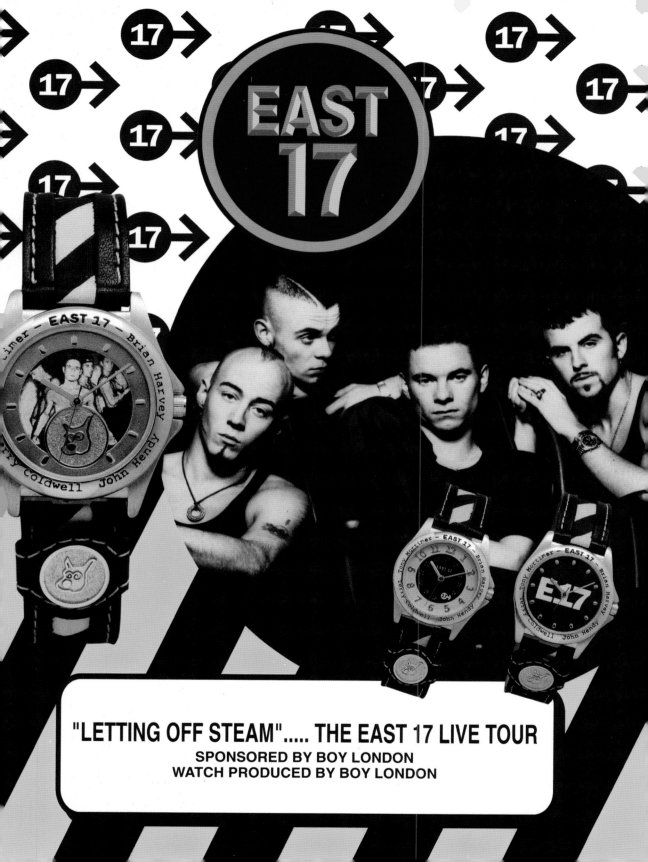

"LETTING OFF STEAM"..... THE EAST 17 LIVE TOUR
SPONSORED BY BOY LONDON
WATCH PRODUCED BY BOY LONDON

What time is it?

The only good thing about doing any kind of business in the Far East is the quality of their manufacturing skills, but the up side pretty much stops right there, especially if you care especially about the artistry and creativity. They always seemed to rip the heart and soul outta what it was you were aiming for.

Take my BOY watches as a prime example. These watches were amazing and the packaging we came up with meant they were even more unique. They pushed the brutal, sadomasochism of my aggressive, adrenaline fuelled clothing label into new territory. They complimented the hard metal and black that BOY was now famous for and helped us survive the move from Punk and the New Romantics. With sharp designs in metal and an almost sci-fi watch face that harped back to BOY's black and metal Punk roots mixed with the industrial design of my original PX shop. The entire concept was a showstopper and everybody who was anyone wanted one. They were stellar and fitted right in with the new age of the 90's. They were unique and only BOY could have produced them. The logo was stamped into the metal as well as the leather or metal strap. The faces came in hundreds of different designs, some popped open, some had swivelling dials, it was extreme styling. We even made watches for Elton John complete with a metal dog tag and packaged in a metal flight case. The publicity around them was huge and we started selling them big time, nothing could stop us.

Boy George once said that the BOY watches were our downfall and he was spot on. This was the 80's and on the one hand it was going great for us but the downside was we had entered the business world and it's a world full of disgusting people in suits handing out business cards. It was a long, long way from the Sex Pistols and the Punk era and I fucking hated them all. It was not my world.

Worse still, this was when the Far East first got their hands on BOY. When I say our watches were unique that was true in the West, but from Singapore to South Korea it became the exact opposite. Factories there were manufacturing 1000s of copies per day for everybody and anybody and they certainly didn't give a fuck what brand they stamped onto them. Before I knew it copies of our watches were everywhere and it turned out the factories making them were run by the fucking Asian mafia, so it seemed I was now unintentionally in the mafia watch bizness. So paradoxically our success was our failure.

I designed a pair of shoes once which I had manufactured in a factory in Northampton. By the way if you've ever been to Northampton I'm sure it's a memory you choose to forget! I hated the place… So, I went to loads of trouble to design these shoes and get them made. They were called The Jam Shoe, and they were a well-crafted black and white shoe based on the Mod style as worn by The Jam….While the factory was busy making the order up for me the manager of one of the main shoe stores in Oxford Street just happened to be visiting the factory and spotted my shoes. Now obviously he was a big client and also owned half of the factory, so he had a word with the boss and said "slip a couple of thousands of those 'Jam Shoes' into ourshops but don't tell Stephane". So, the next thing I knew was my designs were all over Oxford Street even before my order arrived with me and that shoe sold in the thousands…

This same scenario happened to me regularly in various places around the world. It was hard to avoid working with unscrupulous factories. It was bad enough having to deal with the catch 22 scenario which was typical of the fashion industry. This would involve wanting to get a great design produced in small quantities in order to keep the pieces unique therefore not wanting to commit to an order of 1,000's. Unfortunately, it was literally impossible to source a factory that would produce such small numbers, and even if it was possible it would be far too expensive leaving no margin for profit. To make matters worse in my case if by some miracle I did manage to finally launch a new collection the whole bloody lot would be copied within moments by the exact type of factory I wanted to use in the first place!

Here's a heads up for any fashion students reading this, there's nothing you can do about any of it unless you buy a gun or find lawyers who are bigger and more expensive than their lawyers. I have probably been copied and ripped off more than any other label over the years and I've heard many naive comments from followers asking why I didn't put a stop to it. Here's why.......

When I was working with a company in LA, or shall we say attempting to, I had my first encounter with Californian lawyers, a situation I will always regret. I learned very quickly that none of this was for me. So, these LA trade mark lawyers who we employed to chase and secure our BOY trademarks around the world would meet me and produce a map of the world which they would stick on my wall, they would then point out the blue dots which represented BOY and the red dots which represented the enemy. The enemy being people who had registered the BOY name unlawfully. They informed me one day of a case where the dictator of some small fucking country somewhere was demanding $20,000 to return the BOY trade mark to us. The problem was the lawyers only solution for dealing with this particular problem was to instruct the rebel army of that country to kill the dictator, thus saving us loads of money!

When I then found out that my legal fees per year were over $1,000,000 USD my accountant suggested that I would be better off closing down all global activities and just keeping the place on Kings Road, Chelsea. He told me I would actually make more money that way, but of course by now we were in so deep with the men from LA that it was hard to unravel any of it. It became fucking clear to me that not one of them, apart from my accountant, was to be trusted. In the end the chaos that was caused meant that my favourite quote 'I DECIDED TO OPEN A SHOP CALLED BOY AND CAUSE TROUBLE', was quite apt!

Hey, we're going to Ibiza

I don't know if I was permanently on one but my highs were always higher than many of the people around me back then especially seeing as I wasn't using at the time. I was just naturally high. I never knew what everyone else was on, H, E's, Crack, MDMA, K, Cocaine. It was all around me. I mean everybody I knew was on something, loads of people that worked for me were taking something or started to once they became part of the system. Some ended up in an even worse situation by turning into major drug dealers. A few liked the fact that I was in NA and AA and would hang out with me just to get back to being healthy. Some died. I was in my own space and zone.

At the time I had my office in Barcelona, I was also supplying stock to the place in the gay quarter of Sitges and I had the villa in St Tropez. It was all sufficient to keep me interested but I really wanted to branch out to Ibiza. It was only a boat ride away and it was the 'summer of love' and everyone was going to be there. I enjoyed the boat trip, there was acid house playing day and night, a swimming pool on board, it was steaming hot weather and dolphins were following the boat, what was not to like? I arrived and hit the streets of Ibiza when it was getting dark and the first thing I noticed was a wall of sound coming from everywhere, cafes, restaurants, bars, cars with their doors flung open with no one inside! It was an orchestra of sounds. I was on the cool side of Ibiza with clubs like KU, Space, Manumission and Amnesia. I wondered what the other side of the island was like, I'd heard it had bars like the pub on EastEnders....

As soon as I walked into KU I was feeling it. Even the parking lot was crazy, there must have been 50 staff with torches parking the cars but it was nothing short of organised chaos! The club was fucking amazing, it was immense and there were thousands on the dance floor. The roof was open as it was a hot night, the swimming pool looked perfect. I climbed to the top of one of the speakers and dived into the crowd, my arms outstretched. Before long a mirror image of myself appeared in front of my face, it was another party goer wearing a straw hat and mimicking all my moves, I soon realized that this was what Ibiza was all about and it felt brilliant. It was all my best experiences with clubbing going right back to the Mod days, all rolled into one. The crescent moon was shining down through the open roof and I said to the girl that was with me, "this is as good as it gets".

Ibiza is full of girls at rooftop bars now, looking dumb, taking selfies, going on clubbing holidays but too fucking late and they only go now because it's safe, happy clubbing. Clubbing is supposed to be edgy and slightly dangerous, some of the best night's I've ever had ended up in trouble. Occasionally a club wouldn't let me in, a few times they wouldn't even let me in to my own party! Once a gang of us were on the road to a club in Manchester but we got lost after taking too much speed and ended up in a field full of sheep. Even when I was on the guest list, which was most of the time, I would join the line of punters who were hoping to get in, my expectations were never that high cos I knew as soon as I was in the whole thing was over. They say go late leave early.......

Ebeneezer good

Not long after my first visit to Ibiza I organised a take-over and fashion show with the owners of KU club, I called it 'No Sleep till London'. I can't even remember going or who came with me now but somehow, we all got there. The entire BOY army was there including models and dancers and it starred Wild Child. She was a precocious 14-year-old, girl and had been given the name Wild Child after she hit the front covers of the British tabloids because of the scandal she caused at my fashion show and party which was held at the notorious Limelight club in Oxford Circus, London.

With this particular show Fat Tony was on DJ duties and I'd had the idea to let the models get as smashed and mashed as possible before going on stage. I wanted to create a very British fashion show that was the polar opposite of the French and Italian shows of the fashion houses in Paris and Milan. I used my artistic licence to turn the BOY shows into total anarchy!

So I let them all loose and the result was models with no panties on falling off the stage and Wild Child gate crashing the show, ripping her clothes off and stripping completely naked in front of a full house! Later that night there was a sex party in the dressing room and the whole event became infamous within the fashion world!

BOY was the darling of the club scene back then and after this event and with our ever-growing profile we could fill a London venue ten times over, so now here we were taking over IBIZA!

KU was no small nightclub and it looked like thousands of clubbers had turned up, so to get the party started in front of this huge crowd, the models came out two by two as the KU house DJs played Strip for Me, I'll Strip for You. The models and dancers were wearing the notorious BOY flag outfits, to spice the show up they started to throw off their clothing, the crowd started shrieking 'off, off'!, so off came their clothes! For the finale everybody jumped fucking naked into the huge swimming pool in front of the stage.

The day after the show we headed back to the hotel just as dawn was rising with its morning chorus of drum and bass and furniture being chucked into the swimming pool. We needed to get some zeds, which was pretty difficult in Ibiza any time of day and night. We woke around midday, I put the roof down on the car and off we drove to the other side of the island and found a private Ibiza cove. We needed to relax on the beach by a cool beach bar for the afternoon. We met up with some of the model boys who were grooving to the chilled out sounds and the afternoon turned into a mellow, mini rave. The beach was littered with sunbeds and bodies and right in the middle, entertaining the naked sun worshippers was Wild Child.

'Stephane Raynor is a mad genius! His vision for fashion was and is before any of our time. My aunt Ramesh is a famous Persian singer who mixed Punk with royalty! Growing up I would just wait for her to come to the States from London to see what she had bought me from BOY. Her style was everything..... BOY was everything. Fast forward to the present day when my best friend Sam Sarpong (RIP) began modelling for BOY... it never left me... came back full circle, stronger than ever!'

Sammy Amiransari - Sr Talent Producer (Project Runway Jr.)

2000s

Damaged goods
(Rants, Raves and Revolutions)

40 years on and people still talk about their lives being changed forever after their first association with BOY. A while ago I was seeing a beautiful Italian girl who looked like Sophia Loren, she was designing with me at the time and one day she said, 'your shops are like a spider's web, and you can trap whoever you want'. Another time a boy cried, 'can I get another BOY cap quick, I lost mine last night fucking someone'. A girl came into BOY and declared 'Look at me, I'm damaged goods, I saw a boy in a club wearing a BOY T-shirt so I fucked him!'. The guy on the door of Studio 54 called out 'hey you in the BOY shirt, come in'. Debbie Harry cited BOY as her favourite shop and put a photo of it in her book.

This was my work, my job, my life. Always creating a magical world of imagination and adventure, for this was how I lived my life and I wanted and needed to share it, the world can be such a dull uneventful place and so for an entrepreneur like me it was necessary to turn my dreams into a reality and play games with people's minds by giving them exactly what they wanted before they even KNEW they wanted it.

One thing I regret more than any other is not spending as much time in BOY as I could have, but that aside I was so passionate about my creations that I always felt personally responsible for them, 24 hours a day. I was blessed with this life changing opportunity to design and actually create a world of fantasy and to be allowed to live in it. So, for a Leicester kid with absolutely no education this was a gift from God.

A Listers

It's almost an impossibility to stay current but that's always been my goal. I've also had the entire world of pop stars wanting to wear my cult fashion labels for the past 40 years which is something very special.

There was something I did back in 1973 that made all this happen and so began the story of my legendary rise to fame. Rumours and stories of the underground set that gathered around me which included Patti Smith, Chrissie Hynde, Mr Marley, the Depeche boys, Thomson Twins, Generation X and Pete Burns, got bigger and wilder as my reputation grew. These stories led to the likes of Madonna and Rihanna to also believe in my label along with all the celebs of the club scene and dance floor.

A true altruist, I've never sold out but always kept the faith, eating, sleeping, living and loving what I do. I love the world I'm in but to dare not step outside its boundaries. My body of work is hard to describe as I've always been running 20 years ahead of everybody else and I often paid a high price, being envied and copied. I've suffered my crown of thorns to be taken and used by the unscrupulous, the thief's snakes and serpents, in a cruel world where I don't belong.

I'm not a commodity
(Rants, Raves and Revolutions)

When I started out there wasn't a city financial investment culture and nobody was looking for smart new investments so I didn't think about it at the time, in fact I didn't think about it at all. Since then however the financial world has been looking for anything they can hang their hat on and get for a fucking killing. Greed and capitalism had started to grow around me as I climbed, or rather hurtled towards success. I never really fell into any predictable format, instead I was pushing and pulling the fashion industry apart. I was an angry young man, like Joe Orton, or a younger David Bailey. I was wild, mad and crazy and I did anything I wanted. I wanted to get my own way and I didn't take any prisoners. I had been a Mod; a top face and it's been said that if you're a Mod you are always right. I think it's something to do with wearing the sharpest handmade suits, shirts and ties with a polka dot handkerchief in the top pocket. A Mod was simply a cut above everyone else.

I had polarised everyone and everything around me, I was experimental and always moving things around. Once I had established a new shop and it had become successful I was already on to the next one and taking it in a different direction. I would freeze moments in time, like shape shifting, I was a minimalist, a composer of the Avant Garde, a gun for hire. I would shoot straight and talk straight although I never knew I talked differently to everyone else until people started saying it. I was crowned by The Times newspaper as the 'Marks and Spencer of Punk'. I was certainly an instigator of much of British youth culture. Acme Attractions was considered one of the coolest shops on the planet, as was PX in Covent Garden. I was a "situationist", I loved creating things that had never been done before, rejecting everything that was considered normal and acceptable in everyday society.

Now I am finally being given credit for much of the emergence of gay culture. It wasn't that hard to do as it was in my DNA having had many notorious relationships with the girls AND boys around me. There was decadence, glamour, fashion and fun to be had everywhere. My days started late and went on into the dead of night of the London club scene.

I was passionate about French and Italian film noir. I've played with art and fashion all my life and it seems as though further generations have finally turned into what I was responsible for creating. I had made a revolutionary attack on society and the fashion industry with my gender role play through fetish wear and fetish clubs. I didn't anticipate my impact on everything around me but I knew something was going on, I just knew. I've used my life to challenge and change what I saw around me. It was a response and reason to live, to stay alive, to stay one step beyond. I lived at breakneck speed. I'm an experimentalist, I never look back and I have a disregard for sentimentality. I've hardly had any friends, they just pull you back or get in the way. With my attitude and my love for life and art I would never have been able to handle working in an office. The speed of my mind has kept me wanting more passion, more craziness, more fun, more smashing down of doors. Never turn me into a commodity as that's when the fun stops.

Out of Anarchy Comes Creativity.

East is East

I took over LALA London completely in 2001 and moved the business one block along towards the corner of Lamb Street. This unit had an entrance at the front and back, with the back leading straight into Spitalfields Market, which meant there was customer traffic coming in from both ends. The market was amazing back then. There were farm animals, a football pitch and a swimming pool but no supermarkets or shops. These were early days for the market and surrounding area and it was a very long way from Chelsea and Covent Garden. Something was telling me that East London was about to take off, the West End was definitely moving east. I remembered when I lived in Chelsea I hated going to East London but by now I could see it more clearly and for some reason I was feeling more at home there.

My work was changing and I had decided to be more of an architect of life. I realised there were plenty of young professionals buying up loft apartments. Everything was up for grabs and if you bought property back then you'd be very wealthy now. I had a call from Tower Hamlets Council the day after they had seen me on the front of The Sunday Times and offering me a 5 storey loft building in Shoreditch for £6,000. I thought here we go again, and with Prince singing it's 1999 I knew I was onto something, but I needed to change my style, like a chameleon, and morph into this new playground. I realized I could turn back time to the days of fitting out PX and even further back to Acme Attractions and once again get involved with furniture design. I started to do some serious business, I was selling 10 seat modular vintage leather sofas, arch Italian lamps, vintage coffee tables and objet d'art. I even started buying up old Space Invaders and Donkey Kong arcade games, both full size and pub table versions. Early hipsters and graphic artist were coming over to buy from me for their cool new East End lofts. I was getting known by all the top interior designers as they were coming in to buy for their wealthy clients. I started kitting out complete interiors for all the East End bars like Match, Light Bar and Medicine Bar. I even made it into the design book of the year.

I was also buying up Solex mopeds from France, the type with the little engines mounted on the front. Libertines' Pete Doherty had one and he used to pull up on it when he came to LALA London to nick everything. Once he walked out with a retro synth organ under his jacket and a bunch of other stuff but I really liked him, he was well cool and, in any case, he'd come back every Thursday and pay for what he nicked the week before! I also sold vintage Peugeot racing bikes, I had around 30 at one point, and I became London's premier vintage bike store years before anyone else. I was made up. Finally, I added a vintage clothing store in the basement, and off I went again, full circle….

As with everything I'd done before, I'd hit the streets of Spitalfields very early on and during the 5 years it became safe for the followers to slowly creep in so I had to leave because the area went ballistic and rents soared. In 2007 I moved to one of the worst streets near Brick Lane, called Redchurch Street and I called my shop Sick. Nobody walked down this street either by day or night but as always I loved it because it was falling down and there was graffiti everywhere, it was a gangsta wasteland with crack gangs around the corner and no street lights. I saw someone get stabbed there once, funny thing is I found out later that some of my staff were dealing drugs from the shop, I'd always wondered why the gangs left us alone, I guess it was outta respect. So, I set up shop and waited for the arrival of the next wave of youth culture and sure enough they turned up in their skinny black jeans, reading Vice magazine and checking their MySpace profiles! To cut a long story short it's now the trendiest street in London and Gucci have just moved in!

Sometimes it's just right. Working for Stephane at BOY was my right. Crazy, fun-filled days, being part of groundbreaking fashion history were the best times of my life. I wouldn't change a thing. BOY was my entire life. It shaped so many others lives around the world, and I was so lucky to be part of such a fashion culture revolution. I'm privileged to be part of Stephane's story, which needs to be told. Exciting, crazy times, we were untouchable. We were BOY.

Angie Usher

2010s

Meltdown

In 2012 a stylist came into my Sick shop in London's East End, it was a pop-up shop I'd put together just to create some diversity. This stylist was looking for something unusual for her client to wear, and after talking with her for a while I discovered the outfit was for RiRi to wear for a well know television show she was appearing on that weekend. After much discussion we decided that I would create an outfit for her with the criteria of 'something special and unique'. I suggested that my team produce an original Stephane Raynor creation that I had originally designed in the 1980's. The outfit consisted of a turtleneck top, RA RA skirt, leggings and cap all very clearly covered in the iconic BOY logo. The entire outfit could be classed as a replica vintage design.

We were given information about the show by the producers and they sent us quite definite instructions about the strict laws surrounding product advertising. That was also when we found out that RiRi would be wearing the outfit for her interview with Jonathon Ross! Jonathan's show is one of the biggest weekend television chat shows watched by millions every week. So, we had a problem as the law states that no clothing can display brand logos or advertising which could contravene product placement laws.

RiRi's outfit was deemed to be vintage so we hoped that would mean we might get away with it! By now she was a massive star in the U.K and millions of avid viewers were waiting to see her first ever appearance on British TV and she was due to be live on set for the whole hour. She was within minutes of going live when the shit hit the fan. Someone had spotted that she was dressed head to toe in BOY which was of course full on product advertising, which as I said was not allowed under any circumstances! The problem was heightened by the urgency of live TV. They couldn't blur out the BOY logo as it was all over the fukkin outfit so there was No Way Out! Out she went live in front of the cameras; she moved, danced and virtually sat on Jonathan's lap!

Immediately there was a total Twitter melt down and for many different reasons. Some tweeters were asking how she was able to wear an outfit that was clearly promoting BOY. Other staunch BOY fans were complaining that I had sold out by allowing a star like Rihanna to wear BOY but I also spoke to one of my gay BOY fans who exclaimed "OMG we all loved RiRi in BOY" .... You can't win 'em all.

I just thought it was crazy that I'd managed to fool everyone and got away with it! You can't begin to imagine how I love the fact that BOY caused trouble all over again……

Culture clash

People expect me to be hanging out somewhere in the world, living the dream. A place like Hollywood in a Spanish style villa with a swimming pool, or southern Spain, maybe on an exotic island, or in a glamorous New York duplex, but it's not like that, plus that would be an anti-climax to the book. I recently opened a space in Berlin, a place that's the next bright hope for the future of art and fashion, and now I'm back scouring London's back streets just in case there's anything left here that I can turn into something new and exciting, because for me it's not about the riches and the fame, it's more about what I can come up with next.

I'm even thinking about South America, perhaps following Ronnie Biggs the great train robber. I feel like putting a tent up on a beach in El Salvador or finding a shack in the Favela's of Rio.

For me it's still the Punk ethos cloaked and disguised as fashion. You see the paradox in all of this is that what made BOY great was its failure, the fact that it became successful actually ruined its image. When I ran BOY everyone knew I didn't give a fuck. BOY wasn't about putting the logo on everyone or having a plush office somewhere and a flash business card. I lived my life like a rock and roll band. It was more about what's that cunt gunna come up with next . Some of the best moments of my life have been spent sleeping on the shop floor and dreaming about what mischief I could come up with tomorrow, for 'Tomorrow is Another Day' (Gone with the Wind).

Five years
(Rants, Raves and Revolutions)

The thing is, every five years or so society changes, music changes, fashion changes, technology changes, sexuality changes, politics change, products change, images change, times change, ideas change, people change, relationships change, emotions change, and most certainly the world changes. Everything changes when you're in the world I'm in and I can feel these changes happening. It's a bit like looking in the mirror and watching yourself age. I notice these shifts in social awareness so strongly but these changes of attitude and behaviour will never stop, they are relentless. However, its only possible to avoid many of these changes if your lifestyle is stuck in a time warp. I know people who still only listen to music from the 60's and 70's bands like The Who, The Stones or Zeppelin, they're unable to move on. There are so many people who are stuck in the era they grew up in, who met someone, got married, had babies, got a mortgage a dog and a fucking fridge freezer, the changes I'm talking about won't have had much of an effect on these people..........

Marc Bolan, who like me could see the future, didn't live or even think like others do. The big difference is that most people only look in the mirror when they need to; let's say when they're going out to meet someone, or for a job interview etc. For me, I constantly feel as though I'm inside the mirror, not out of ego or vanity, but just to check I'm still here, or that I actually exist. I never take anything for granted, I live in a world of perpetual change; like Malcolm McLaren, I will change my accent and my voice depending on who's in the room. I'm always changing my image so that people don't recognise me, but more importantly I change my beliefs, attitudes, friends and sexual partners constantly. That's why I like fetish clubs – the idea of having weird sexual encounters and then not remembering who that person was is very satisfying. No attachment at all to anything, it allows my mind to travel, to explore the dangerous, the dark and the unknown and I need to use all these techniques to do what I do. I must NEVER be found to be boring..........

No sell out

My BOY, the one I originally created had a real strength and was founded within a distinct philosophy which was to never let my followers down. If die hard Punks walked in complaining that it was a rip off having to pay £20 for a T-shirt because they knew what they cost me to make, I would find that quite testing as it showed that they placed no value on my time or artistry or the concepts I had worked on over the years.

However, I think it's remarkable that I have even had a following for so long. To me it's on a level with band fandom, in fact BOY has actually outlasted most bands and different genres of music. What a crazy, mad fukkin life I've had, whether it was Rockers, Teddy Boys, Mods, Hippies, Skinheads, Suedeheads, Casuals, Soul Boys, Punks, New Romantics, Goths, Transsexuals, Gay Boys, Fashionistas, Ravers, Brit Pop, Girl Power, Clubbers, Indie Kids or Hipsters I loved it all, dressed it all, did it all and I couldn't stop now even if I wanted to.

My way has always been to never sell out. I turned down most press and publicity and refused to be featured in magazines. Rolling Stone was trying to contact me for some time but I kept ignoring their emails. In the end I agreed to do an interview because I wanted to tell my story.

I never wanted followers of BOY to think I'd betrayed them. There have been times when certain pop stars that the fans disapproved of have worn BOY but it's difficult to choose between brand exposure and fan loyalty. It's funny how these things have become almost political at times, but at the end of the day BOY has always belonged to the people.

Golden years

153 King's Rd London was more than just an address, it represented the golden years of BOY. It really doesn't matter what came afterwards, these were the truly unforgettable years, the years that shaped a legend both for me and for BOY. It was the time in which I became the boy that created BOY. My identity and my DNA are all over it…. The story wouldn't have happened without me and no matter what has happened since BOY's greatest years, both my name and BOY are inextricably linked so that now it's impossible to tear us apart. My early designs have never been bettered, they are strong and send out such a powerful message of hedonism, a rebel yell, a crusading anarchic flag of true rebellion. My work is still seen as relevant and contemporary, it's still laced with the controversy that has shape shifted the brand over 40 years of chaos and disorder, deliberately engineered by me in order to confuse and delight fans of BOY.

In the end, as is the same with so many stories within music and fashion, the words of The Gallagher brothers are spot on when they said that playing to 5,000 hard core fans was fucking brilliant but playing to 50,000 just became boring. I needed to keep ducking and diving between being too blasé, becoming too commercial or worse still, getting bored with the whole thing. I always knew the dangers of change but I took my chances and went from BOY to BOY LONDON thanks to an idea inspired by the Americans. In the same way that when Blondie went from Punk to Disco the change alienated many of their fans but the risk payed off for Blondie in the same way it did for BOY as changing direction lifted both of us to new heights! The change thrust BOY into outta space and it became a global brand overnight. 153 King's Road was packed with people wanting a piece of BOY and those iconic words were subsequently spread far and wide and all over the world.

I've talked about anger, about misunderstanding, my love of the boys and girls that really knew how to wear BOY, those who understand that BOY was not about boys at all, that it was actually a state of mind. It was amazing to watch kids from mixed cults and movement's 'getting' each other, treating the extreme with an air of respect. BOY has a legendary past, it has been a huge influence on four decades of kids but has always been about the future. I recently heard of an up and coming young designer, who's label is called Lover Boy. I'm into the fact that the name and his designs give a nod to the essence of the King's Road days. I hope he also goes on to stir it up and fuck with the fashion business.

BOYL

THE PROPERTY

THE RESU

RRECTION

Another dimension

It's towards the end of the book and I'm struggling for an ending because as you may have gathered and are beginning to understand, I'm not living in the ordinary world and all the things that have happened to me are perhaps not the end but instead only the beginning and now I find I'm on a journey to understand and discover myself.

The pages you have been reading, about everything that's happened to me from the start, as I've repeatedly said, are perhaps not actually about me, or to be more explicit and precise, they were all about another me, because as we go through time our lives, opinions, and relationships change. I allow everything to change even if that means my life may never be the same again. Most people don't want change, they feel threatened by it, but for me it's essential to put myself at risk, to feel the rush of the unknown.

I don't believe in time but I have always been interested in non-linear time, that is to say time that doesn't always move forward. There have been many times in which I've been told I can see the future and predict what's coming next. Because of this skill certain people and business entities have tried to invest in me and my ideas over the years, hoping to get a glimpse of my inner self or perhaps to steal, copy, or trick me into giving away my secrets. The problem is you see, if you invest in yourself you may find you struggle to make money, but if someone invests in you, you may never get paid at all. For me, everything I've done, been, lived and achieved, I now realise was just the beginning, all the music, fashion, sexual orientation and deviation was nothing more than a practice run.

During a recent meeting I had with a business associate it was suggested that the BOY eagle should be replaced by the eagle holding the word GOD, with GOD being a reference to me. A girl I used to be very close to once said to me, "if you're really a genius you must kill yourself, as all great geniuses kill themselves", so we made a plan to do it one day while she photographs it!

I'm older now, my life is rushing before me, memories both good and bad are all the same to me. The movie doesn't always need a happy ending, you don't always get what you want. I see my life as a continuous movie, my own show reel, this is how I've always lived, waiting for the next turn or curve in the road. I've been living in Berlin recently and one evening I was lying on the couch watching the movie Atomic Blonde, a movie set in Berlin, and there in the middle of the fucking movie was a character wearing one of my BOY T-shirts.

I started to think back over my life and it was all rushing through my brain and I concluded that I don't belong anywhere any more. I must escape, there's too much small talk going on, I need to breath. I don't know where I'm going and I'm hating what I should be loving. The next day I got in my car and left. I was tired, felt ill and I was lonely. I decided to head to Paris then on to London hoping I would feel better once I got there. I was driving fast to reach the ferry in time, the headlights picked out a forest, I glanced at the dash board of my car, suddenly the ground underneath the car became unstable, the car was shaking then it slid across the road and smashed straight into a tree! I've often wondered how it would all end…. I guess this wasn't to be it.

Not surprisingly, I've been thinking and talking about the next world for a while. When I watch people today from the window of my new pad on London's Commercial Road in the fashionable East End, all I see are figures scurrying to and from work and I wonder, what do they really know of life? I think about people that I've loved, girls that I once loved from the 70s who were 18 then and are in their 60's now, girls and boys from only as far back as 2007 who are now in their 30's, the music, the fashion and cars that I loved which these days are classed as vintage, or classic and the travel and journeys I loved to go on. Forget The Beatles or The Stones, some young interns of mine have actually asked me who The Spice Girls or Britney Spears are! Sometimes I can't go back at all. I don't want to wade through the clouds of history, it's useless and boring. It doesn't feel like it was me anyway plus I have much better things to do with my time. Occasionally I hear a great track, a sound bite, even a song on a TV advert. I hate the way big companies use classic songs to promote lame products like fucking floor cleaner. It should be stopped now and the culprits destroyed. But then the other side of my brain kicks in as very I'm aware that we live in a world of perpetual motion. The never-ending story that eventually turns to dust. In the future we all end up passing, as time is not our servant.

I've often said I don't believe in history, that history is not stuck in time, it can be linear, it can move sideways, backwards, forwards. I'm an astral traveller, my history is one that comes and goes depending upon my moods and the time in which I'm living, but one thing I don't do is talk about the good old days or feed off reminiscence's, sentimentality, nostalgia or memories.

I once met Bjork and she told me she wanted to change her name to ASTROBOY, which was another label I had been working on at the time. I found it a strange request but now it makes much more sense. So now I'm faced with pushing on to the next level, perhaps realising that life isn't a game. The route I would chose would be to hack my way into the Matrix so I can live with ROBOTS, who really are the future, then morph into ASTROBOY and fly away.

... To be continued. Stephane Raynor

**Written by Stephane Raynor
an Autobiography**

Associate Story Editor: Rhiannon Sussex
Photographic Reproduction Editor: Rick Piercy
Personal Diary: Angie Usher
Book Design: Colin Hagan

Dedicated to my Mother & Father
William Hardy Raynor and
Gladys Violet Sandown Raynor

Love to my Long Lost friend David Parkinson
without whom none of this may have happened.

Special thanks to Rhiannon and Rick for pulling
this book together and preventing murder.

To my dearest friend and personal assistant Angie
Usher. A lifetime award for putting up with me.

Photo Credits
Additional Photography: Paul Gobel, David Parkinson,
Jack English, Paul Everett, Rick Piercy.

Captions and Credits:
Endpaper Illustration: Mark Wigan
Images: p5 BOY Boutique, King's Road, Chelsea.
Homer Sykes Archive / Alamy / p6 Stephane Raynor.
Paul Roundhill / p27 Generation X. Peter Gravelle
/ p28 Ready Steady Go! Badges, 1970s. Mick
Sinclair/Alamy / p30 BOY Poster designed by Peter
Christopherson 1978 / p33 King's Road, 1977. Paul
Revere/REX/Shutterstock / p34 BOY King's Road
1984. Sandra Skies Ludwig / p37 BOY Boutique,
King's Road, Chelsea. Homer Sykes Archive / Alamy
/ p39 BOY Boutique, King's Road, Chelsea. Homer
Sykes Archive / Alamy / p41 Sex Pistols, London,
1977. Trinity Mirror/Mirropix/Alamy / p42, p45, p46,
p47, p48, p49, p50, p51, p232 Artwork by Jamie
Reid / p53 Punks, The Roxy, 1977. Derek Ridgers /
p55 The Roxy, April 1977. Richard Braine / PYMCA /
REX/Shutterstock / p58 Punks, The Roxy, 1977. Derek
Ridgers / p61 Steve Strange and Princess Julia, The
Blitz, Covent Garden, February 1980. Trinity Mirror/
Mirrorpix/Alamy / p62 Stephen Linard, The Blitz, 1980
/ p72 Arches nightclub, Charing Cross, London 1980.

Homer Sykes Archive / Alamy / p76 Steve Strange,
The Blitz, 1979. Derek Ridgers / p99 Princess Julia,
The Blitz, Covent Garden, 13th February 1980. Mike
Lloyd/Daily Mirror/Mirropix / p115 BOY Labels. Phil
Rees/Alamy / p120 Sex, King's Road, December
1976. Trinity Mirror/Mirropix/Alamy / p122 Malcolm
McLaren. Peter Gravelle / p131 Rihanna, Los Angeles,
March 2012. Wenn UK/Alamy / p136 Boy George
and Michael Dunn, Soho 1986. Brendon Beirne/
REX/Shutterstock / p139 Boy George, 1980s. Everett
Collection Inc/Alamy / p151 Pet Shop Boys. Chris van
de Vooren/Sunshine International/REX/Shutterstock /
p154 Hyper Hyper fashion show, October 1988. Paul
Massey/Daily Mirror/Mirropix / p161 BOY Boutique,
King's Road, Chelsea. Homer Sykes Archive / Alamy
/ p164 Bananarama, Bond Street, August 1986.
Ilpo Musto/REX/Shutterstock / p169 The Game,
Hollywood. AKM-GSI / p171 Billy Idol. Peter Gravelle
/ p179 BOY Clothing. Phil Rees/Alamy / p183 Poll
Tax Riots, London 1990. Jim Hodson/Alamy / p201
Holly Johnson and Elton John, Music Therapy Lunch,
London 1990. Richard Young/REX/Shutterstock /
p214 Kendrick Lamar, Hyde Park, Jul 2016. WFPA/
Alamy / p219 Sick, Redchurch Street, London. Tim E.
White/Alamy / p220 Sick Boutique, Redchurch Street,
London. Loop Images Ltd / Alamy / p226 Rihanna on
the Jonathan Ross Show, London, March 2012. Brian
J. Ritchie Photography Ltd/REX/Shutterstock / p229
Punk, June 1977. Trinity Mirror/Mirropix/Alamy / p231
Nicki Minaj in concert at the Peabody Opera House,
St Louis, USA, 31st July, 2012. Startraks Photo/REX/
Shutterstock

Acknowledgement:
Carpet Bombing Culture and Stephane Raynor are
grateful to all the photographers who gave permission
for use of their images in this book. All images are
copyright of their respective owners. While every effort
has been made to contact copyright holders of images,
the author and publishers would be grateful for
information about any images where they have been
unable to trace them, and would be happy to make
amendments in any future editions.